Network Marketing: An Infinite World of Possibilities

(The Ultimate Guide to Network Marketing)

AF519977

Surya Sinha

DIAMOND BOOKS
www.diamondbooks.in

© Author

Publisher	**:**	**Diamond Pocket Books (P) Ltd.** X-30, Okhla Industrial Area, Phase-II New Delhi-110020
Phone	:	011-40712200
E-mail	:	wecare@diamondbooks.in
Website	:	www.diamondbooks.in
Edition	:	2024
Printed By	:	Repro (India)

Network Marketing: An Infinite World of Possibilities
Author - *Surya Sinha*

All rights reserved. No part of this publication may be reproduced, stored in a retrieval system or transmitted in any form or by any means, electronic, mechanical, photocopying, recording or otherwise (except for mentions in reviews or edited excerpts in the media) without the prior permission of the copyright owner.

Contents

1

Network Marketing - An Infinite World of Possibilities

My Purpose of Writing This Book:

When writing this book, I had one primary goal in mind—how can I inspire you to step into the world of network marketing and achieve success in it? This book is not just a simple guide; it is a culmination of my experiences, insights, and emotions, carefully crafted for you in clear and straightforward language.

I understand that network marketing is an exciting yet challenging business. The obstacles you face can sometimes seem daunting, but it is through overcoming these challenges that true growth occurs. In this book, I have not only covered the basics of this business but also addressed the difficulties you may encounter and provided solutions for handling them.

The purpose of this book is to introduce you to the dynamic world of network marketing and to be your trusted companion on this journey. It is designed to help you overcome barriers on your path to becoming a successful network marketer.

Every chapter is written with the intention of making the content easy to understand and applicable to your daily life. Real-life success stories of individuals who have thrived in this business are included, offering lessons learned from their struggles. These stories will help you see that if they can succeed, so can you.

At the end of each chapter, you will find thought-provoking questions designed to encourage reflection on your business and personal growth. These questions are meant to deepen your introspection and guide you in the right direction.

Through this book, I aim to provide you with a comprehensive understanding of network marketing, while motivating you to embrace the challenges and face them head-on. I hope that by the time you finish reading, you will not only feel inspired but also ready to embark on a new chapter of your network marketing journey, propelling yourself toward success.

What's Special About This Book?

1. **Developing the Right Mindset:** The first step to success is cultivating the right mindset. Network marketing requires patience, positivity, and confidence. This book will teach you how to build a mindset that enables you to tackle any challenge and turn obstacles into opportunities. You will learn that mindset is the key that transforms failure into success.

2. **Building an Effective Team:** The essence of network marketing lies in teamwork. While working alone limits your potential, building a strong team multiplies your success. This book will show you how to form an effective team, train them, and foster a winning mindset.

You will also learn how to become a source of inspiration for your team and achieve ambitious goals together.

3. **The Art of Duplication:** Duplication is one of the most important aspects of network marketing. Teaching your team to replicate the same successful system you are using is called duplication. This allows your business to grow rapidly, optimizing your time and efforts. In this book, you will discover simple and effective ways to implement duplication, ensuring that your success scales exponentially.

4. **Keeping the Team Motivated:** Building a team is only the first step; keeping that team motivated and aligned with your goals is crucial. This book will teach you how to inspire and energize your team so that they work together with you, driving toward shared success. You will learn the qualities of a true leader and how to develop these traits within yourself, creating an environment where your team is happy, motivated, and productive under your leadership.

This book is designed to be practical and actionable. As soon as you read it, you'll be able to apply its tips, strategies, and techniques to your daily network marketing activities. Not only will these insights help you grow your business, but they will also guide you toward becoming a more successful and influential network marketer.

Who Is This Book For?

This book is for anyone who has entered or is considering entering the field of network marketing. Whether you're a new networker seeking to learn the ropes or an experienced professional looking to take your success to the next level, this book will provide the guidance you need. Each lesson delves deep into the core of network marketing, teaching you how to build a successful business, overcome challenges, and turn every opportunity into a victory.

Final Note:

This book is a comprehensive guide that covers every aspect of network marketing in depth. Along with practical tips and insights, it will provide you with the tools to not only achieve success in your business but also to inspire those who join your team.

Regards

Surya Sinha
Suryasinha101@gmail.com

2

Unlocking the Potential of Network Marketing

Introduction to Network Marketing

Network marketing, also known as multi-level marketing (MLM), is a business model that has become increasingly popular in recent times. It is a method where companies deliver their products or services directly to consumers, bypassing traditional distributors and retail stores. In this model, you sell products through your personal network and can grow your income by recruiting others to join your network.

One unique aspect of network marketing is that you are not working alone; instead, you build and manage your own team. The larger and more efficient your team, the faster your success grows. Both you and your team benefit directly from each member's hard work.

How This Business Works

Network marketing operates through a straightforward and effective process. It has three main components:

- **Sale of Products or Services:** You sell the company's products or services directly to consumers, which becomes your first source of income. The more you sell, the higher your commission.
- **Team Building and Expansion:** This is where the real power of network marketing lies. You recruit new members to your network, train them, and teach them to replicate the process you're following. This is called *duplication*. As your team expands, your income grows. This becomes another key source of income for you.
- **Support and Training:** Success in network marketing doesn't come only from building a team but also from providing guidance and support. When your team members succeed, you also benefit from their success. Therefore, staying connected with your team and continuously providing them with training is essential.

Why Network Marketing is a Great Business

Network marketing is considered an excellent business opportunity in today's world for several reasons:

- **Low Investment, High Return:** Traditional businesses require significant investment, but network marketing allows you to start with minimal capital. You don't need a physical store or a large staff. You can start from home, and as your network grows, so does your income.

- **Flexibility and Freedom:** In network marketing, you control your schedule. You decide when and where to work, making it an ideal business for those seeking independence while managing other responsibilities, such as family.
- **Opportunities for Learning and Growth:** Beyond financial gains, network marketing provides a platform for continuous learning and personal development. You acquire essential skills in leadership, management, communication, and relationship building.
- **Residual Income:** In network marketing, your earnings are not solely dependent on your personal efforts but also on the work of your team. A strong team can generate a consistent source of income, even when you're not actively working—this is often referred to as passive income.
- **Helping Others Succeed:** One of the most rewarding aspects of network marketing is that you not only work for your own success but also help others achieve theirs. By training and supporting your team members, you positively impact their lives.

Network marketing breaks traditional barriers and offers people the opportunity to fulfill their dreams. This book will provide you with the knowledge and tools needed to become a successful network marketer. By starting your journey with this book, you're paving a new path, not just for yourself, but for everyone who will join you along the way.

Let's embark on this journey together and unlock the endless possibilities that network marketing offers!

Network marketing not only offers financial freedom but also opens up new opportunities and possibilities. By putting in consistent effort, you can not only enhance your financial situation but also grow both your team and yourself. It is a platform where you can turn your dreams into reality.

3

Basic understanding of network marketing

Network marketing is a business model where you don't just sell products but also expand your network by bringing new people into your team. This unique model allows you to sell products through your personal connections while growing the business by recruiting others. One of the key reasons for its popularity is the low startup cost and the potential to earn more through consistent effort and strong networking skills. To succeed in this system, it is crucial to select the right products, develop effective sales techniques, and build a robust network. This business presents a significant opportunity for individuals looking to create a successful career through their hard work.

Understanding Network Marketing and Its Structure:

Network marketing is a business model where companies rely on independent distributors to sell their products or services directly to customers. As a distributor, you not only sell products but also recruit others to join your network, encouraging them to grow within the business. The distinguishing feature of this model is that you earn income both from your personal sales and commissions from the sales generated by your team. Through this structure, you have the potential to double your earnings by leveraging your own efforts and the expansion of your network, which continues to increase your income over time.

Real Example: Savita Agnihotri was an ordinary woman who started her journey in network marketing by selling products to her friends and family. Initially, she earned a modest income, which she found satisfactory. However, once she understood the true potential of network marketing, her approach transformed. She introduced her friend Rahul to the business, and Rahul, in turn, added his own network of friends. As Savita's team gradually grew, she began earning commissions not just from her own sales but also from the sales made by Rahul and his team. In this way, Savita's income multiplied. This illustrates the core strength of network marketing—benefiting from both individual and team efforts, leading to continuous income growth.

Selling Products and Services:

The most essential step in network marketing is the sale of products or services. In this business model, you directly connect with customers, providing them with detailed information about the products. Unlike traditional retail businesses, you establish a personal relationship with the customer. This personal connection not only boosts sales but also helps maintain long-term business stability. When customers trust your products, it fosters lasting relationships, allowing your business to grow steadily.

Real-Life Story: Suman Srivastava, a simple housewife, spent most of her time caring for her family. One day, she discovered an opportunity in network marketing, selling health products. Initially, Suman sold these products to her family, neighbors, and friends. Along with the sales, she guided her customers on how to use the products effectively, focusing not just on making sales but on offering real solutions to their health concerns. Over time, her reputation for reliability and honesty grew in her community. Customers not only came to her for the products but also for her advice and support. As her customer base expanded, Suman's sales increased, and she realized that network marketing was not just about business but about building a community through helping people. This experience boosted her confidence, and she decided to take her network marketing business to new heights. Today, Suman is a successful network marketer, making a lasting impact in her field.

Building and Expanding Your Network:

The key to success in network marketing lies in building a network. Your success depends on how many people you recruit and how well you train them. As you expand your network, each person you add becomes a part of your business, following the same process of selling products and recruiting new members.

This process is known as *duplication.* In duplication, your team members replicate the strategies and techniques you use to grow their own network. As the network expands, so does your business. The benefit of this model is that it relies on the collective efforts of your team rather than on your individual efforts alone. By building a strong team and providing the right training, network marketing leads to long-term success.

Real Example: Ajay Verma started his network marketing journey with personal sales but soon realized that his earnings were limited. After receiving advice from his mentor, Ajay understood that the real path to success was building his own team. He introduced his friend Neelam Patil to the business, and she, too, saw the opportunity and started building her network. Neelam's efforts, combined with Ajay's guidance, helped her build a team of dedicated members. Over time, Ajay's network grew to include more than a thousand people, each working independently to grow their business. This not only brought financial rewards to Ajay but also allowed his network to spread across the country. Ajay's success is a testament to the power of teamwork and network expansion in achieving success in this business.

Future Potential and Business Expansion:

Network marketing is a business with immense potential. You can start small and gradually scale it to new heights. Your earnings are directly linked to the expansion of your network—the larger your network, the greater your income. There are no limits in this business, and with hard work and the right strategies, you can achieve long-term success. Network marketing offers a path to a successful and independent career, where your success is driven by your efforts.

Real-Life Story: Rajesh Kushwaha, hailing from a small village in Bihar, began his career in network marketing. In the early days, he faced numerous challenges, as his network was limited. However, he remained persistent and slowly started building connections. Rajesh expanded his network through personal contacts and effectively utilized social media and digital platforms. Over time, his network spread across the country, and his income reached new heights. Today, Rajesh Kushwaha is a successful entrepreneur and an inspiration to many in the field of network marketing. His journey shows that with perseverance and the right strategy, anyone can achieve remarkable success in this business.

Conclusion

Network marketing offers the opportunity to benefit from both your own efforts and those of your network. This model provides dual earning potential—you not only sell products but also grow the business by adding new members to your team. As your team succeeds, your success grows alongside theirs. To achieve success in this business, it's essential to have the right mindset, patience, and effective strategies.

In today's digital age, the future of network marketing is even brighter. With social media and online platforms, you can connect with people worldwide, making your network limitless. Network marketing provides financial freedom, time freedom, and countless opportunities for personal growth. The more effort and planning you invest, the faster you will progress toward success.

Reflective Questions for Personal and Business Growth

1. **What is network marketing?**
   - Explain the model of network marketing in your own words.
2. **Selling Products and Building a Network**
   - What products have you sold so far, and how have you sold them?

Basic understanding of network marketing

- How many people have you included in your network, and how did you motivate them?

3. **Long-Term Goals**
   - How do you plan to expand your network?
   - How much do you want to grow your network in the next six months?

4. **Network Marketing in the Digital Age**
   - Have you used social media or other digital tools for your business? If yes, what was the result?

5. **Personal Growth**
   - What challenges have you faced in your business, and what have you learned from them?

Final Message

The road to success in network marketing may be challenging, but it is entirely achievable. Every successful network marketer today has faced rejection, struggles, and obstacles in the beginning. Their persistence, patience, and dedication kept them moving forward. These stories of success show that setbacks and failures are simply steps to reaching greater heights.

Their journeys remind us that with patience, determination, and a strong mindset, success in this business is inevitable. They are not only enjoying their success today but are also inspiring others, teaching them that with consistent effort, success is within reach.

You, too, can achieve your dreams—take that first step, move forward with small but steady progress, and remember that success awaits those who never give up. Your future is in your hands—start today to create it!

4

Success Mindset

The most crucial element for success in network marketing is a strong and positive mindset. Your thoughts, attitude, and outlook determine how far you will progress in this business. The right mindset equips you with the strength to face difficulties, boosts your confidence, and prepares you to tackle challenges. When your mindset is positive, you can turn every obstacle into an opportunity and continue moving forward.

The Need for a Positive Mindset

A positive mindset doesn't just mean staying happy or smiling through difficulties; it means finding solutions in every situation. In network marketing, challenges and rejections are inevitable, but with a positive attitude, you will be able to find ways to overcome these obstacles. This mindset ensures that you stay motivated and focused on your goals rather than getting discouraged. A positive outlook helps you see opportunities in every difficulty, allowing you to make progress toward success.

Real Example: Reema Sen began her career in network marketing with great enthusiasm, but she faced several challenges in the early days. Many potential customers rejected her offers, which could have been discouraging. However, instead of feeling disheartened, Reema maintained a positive mindset. She viewed these rejections not as failures but as opportunities to learn and improve.

Reema took valuable lessons from every rejection and worked on refining her skills. She realized the importance of understanding customer needs and building personal connections. By continuously improving her strategies and keeping a positive attitude, Reema's efforts began to bear fruit. Her hard work and positive mindset eventually led her to succeed in network marketing.

Today, Reema Sen is one of the top performers in her company, having built a strong and motivated team. Her story illustrates how a positive mindset and persistent effort can transform rejections into stepping stones for success.

Believing in Yourself

Believing in yourself is the foundation for success in network marketing. When you have faith in your abilities, you are prepared to face challenges head-on. In this business, you will often encounter rejection, competition, and setbacks, but self-confidence empowers you to keep moving forward. When you believe in yourself, others are inspired by your confidence, making them more likely to join you. Your positive thinking and perseverance also influence those around you. Moreover, self-confidence encourages you to adopt new strategies, improve your skills, and continue learning.

Self-belief not only strengthens your leadership skills in network marketing but also paves the way for long-term success.

Real Example: Ankit Bose, a young man from Raipur, decided to pursue a career in network marketing. Initially, he had doubts about whether he could succeed in this field. His family and friends discouraged him, claiming the business was unstable. However, Ankit chose to believe in himself and press forward despite the doubts.

Ankit thought, "If others can succeed in this business, why can't I?" He celebrated even his small successes, which boosted his confidence. His hard work and determination motivated him to keep going, and over the time, his team expanded. His business grew rapidly due to his networking skills.

Today, Ankit Bose is a successful network marketer who overcame his doubts and challenges. His journey is a testament to the power of self-belief and is an inspiration to anyone who may not yet fully trust in their own abilities.

Facing Challenges and Overcoming Difficulties

Challenges are a natural part of network marketing. Many people face rejection, failure, and slow progress in this business. Sometimes, potential clients will decline your offer, or your efforts may not yield immediate results. However, those who succeed in this field are the ones who confront these challenges rather than running from them. Successful people learn from every failure, constantly improving their approach based on their experiences. While difficulties are inevitable, it is how you respond to them that truly matters. By adopting a positive mindset and facing challenges head-on, you can move closer to your goals.

See challenges as opportunities for growth, and use them to learn and evolve. This mindset will lead to long-term success in network marketing.

Real Example: Sunil Kumar, a network leader from Nagpur, worked tirelessly for a year without achieving the level of success he had hoped for. Many of his friends and relatives declined to join his business, leaving Sunil discouraged. Despite the setbacks, Sunil did not give up. He saw these rejections as a challenge and began thinking about what he could improve.

Sunil reassessed his strategy and started trying new approaches. He refined his presentation style, began using social media effectively, and worked on building personal connections with his customers. Slowly but surely, positive results began to emerge, and his hard work paid off. Today, Sunil leads a large and successful team, and he shares his insights with others on how to overcome challenges in network marketing and succeed.

The Power of Self-Motivation

Self-motivation is an essential quality in network marketing. When you are passionate and dedicated to your work, you don't need external encouragement to keep moving forward. Self-motivation means being driven by your own goals and continuously working towards them, regardless of whether someone is pushing you. It allows you to stay focused and achieve success without external pressure. A self-motivated individual progress towards their goals even in the face of challenges.

Real Example: Maya Dixit, a housewife from Bhopal, had always prioritized taking care of her family. When she decided to join network marketing, she initially doubted whether she could succeed given her responsibilities. However, instead of giving up, Maya motivated herself. She resolved to achieve success in network marketing through hard work and determination.

Maya started by dedicating a little time each day to expanding her network, balancing her family responsibilities with her business. Gradually, her efforts began to pay off, and today, Maya leads her own successful team.

Now financially independent and self-reliant, Maya's story is an inspiration to women who want to pursue their dreams while managing their family responsibilities.

Conclusion

The mindset of success is the foundation upon which your entire network marketing business is built. A positive attitude, belief in oneself, the ability to face challenges, and self-motivation are the qualities that will not only make you successful in this business but will also help you grow into a strong leader.

When you believe in yourself and maintain a positive mindset, success is inevitable. Challenges may temporarily block your path, but with the right mindset, you can overcome them and achieve your goals.

In network marketing, your thoughts and attitude are your most valuable assets. By using them wisely, you can accomplish everything you set out to achieve.

Reflective Questions for Personal and Business Growth

1. **Positive Mindset:**
   - What does a positive mindset mean to you, and how will you apply it in your life?
   - Think of a recent challenge—how could you have resolved it with a more positive approach?

2. **Self-Belief:**
   - What steps are you taking to build confidence in yourself?
   - Share an example of a time when self-belief helped you handle a difficult situation.
3. **Facing Challenges:**
   - What recent challenge did you face, and what did you learn from it?
   - How will you handle a similar challenge next time?
4. **Self-Motivation:**
   - How do you keep yourself motivated? What self-motivation tips do you apply in your daily routine?
   - When was a time you needed self-motivation the most, and how did you maintain it?

Final Message

"Your mindset is your guide."

People like Reema, Ankit, Sunil, and Maya were ordinary individuals, but they possessed extraordinary qualities—a positive attitude, belief in themselves, and self-motivation. These traits led them to success. When the road seems difficult, just take one more step forward. Every failure strengthens your experience, and every challenge enhances your abilities.

You can achieve whatever you believe in. All you need is faith in yourself.

5

Ethics and Integrity: Keys to Network Marketing Success

Network marketing is a business where the more you connect with people and build relationships, the greater your chances of success. However, success in this business requires more than just meeting people and sharing information about your products. To truly excel as a network marketer, it is essential to uphold strong ethics and honesty. These values are the foundation for building trust with your customers and team members, which is crucial for long-term success.

Why Ethics and Honesty Matter

Ethics and honesty mean that you provide accurate, truthful information to your customers and team members, without any deception or misleading claims. When you share correct information, your customers begin to trust you and the products you offer. This trust is not only long-lasting but also crucial for the stability of your business.

In network marketing, some individuals may resort to dishonest methods to make quick money, such as exaggerating the benefits of products or making false promises. While these tactics may bring short-term gains, they cannot guarantee long-term success. Sustainable growth in network marketing is built on integrity. By offering honest advice and putting your customers' best interests first, you create loyalty and encourage repeat business.

Building and Maintaining Trust with Customers

Establishing trust with your customers is key to success in network marketing. Once a customer trusts you, they are more likely to not only purchase from you but also refer others to your business.

Here are some essential ways to build and maintain trust with your customers:

- **Provide Accurate Information:** Always give truthful and accurate information about your products. If a product has any side effects, inform your customers about them. This shows that you genuinely care about their well-being and not just making a sale.
- **Listen to Customer Concerns:** If a customer has an issue, listen to them attentively and try to resolve their problem. This is one of the most effective ways to build trust and establish long-term relationships.
- **Work with Integrity:** Avoid making false promises or commitments to your customers. Only promise what you can realistically deliver. This honest approach helps create a positive image of you in the minds of your customers.

Building Trust with Team Members

It is equally important to work with honesty and ethics when dealing with your team members. When your team trusts you, they are more likely to stay with you and work together for the long haul.

- **Maintain Open Communication:** Always keep an open line of communication with your team. Listen to their concerns and guide them in the right direction with transparency.
- **Offer Support:** Be there for your team when they need assistance. When your team members see that you are genuinely supporting them, their trust in you will grow.
- **Provide Proper Training:** Give your team accurate and ethical training so they can also work with honesty and integrity. This creates a positive environment within the team and sets everyone up for success.

Ethics and Honesty: The Keys to Long-Term Success

In network marketing, ethics and honesty are the cornerstones of lasting success. By working with integrity, both with your customers and your team members, you can build strong, long-lasting relationships. These relationships not only drive your business forward but also help you establish a reputation as a trustworthy and respected network marketer.

When people trust you, they will continue to stay by your side and contribute to the growth of your business. Therefore, to become a successful network marketer, it is vital to uphold ethics and honesty in everything you do.

Reflective Questions for Personal and Business Growth

1. **Honesty with Customers and Team Members:**
   Question: Do you always work honestly with your customers and team members?
   ❍ Yes / No
2. **Problem-Solving:**
   Question: When was the last time you listened to a problem from one of your customers or team members and resolved it?
   ❍ Answer
3. **Product Information Transparency:**
   Question: Do you provide information about both the advantages and limitations of your products?
   ❍ Yes / No
4. **Transparency with Team Members:**
   Question: How transparent is your communication with your team members?
   ❍ Very / Medium / Low

Final Message

"Your integrity is your greatest asset."

Long-term success in network marketing requires a commitment to ethics and honesty. When you treat your customers and team members with integrity, you earn their trust, and that trust leads to enduring success. Always remember, work done with honesty and ethics will propel you to great heights.

6

Setting Clear and Achievable Goals

In network marketing, setting clear and achievable goals is critical for success. Goals give your business a clear direction and keep you motivated. When you work with a specific purpose, you know where you are heading and what actions to take to get there. Without goals, navigating the business world is like embarking on a journey without a map - you risk losing your way or taking much longer to reach your destination.

When setting goals, ensure they are realistic and measurable. For instance, if your goal is to add 10 new customers in a month, break it down into smaller tasks and track your progress daily. This approach helps you stay focused and moves you steadily toward your larger goal.

Working with well-defined goals significantly increases your chances of success in network marketing.

The Importance of Setting Goals

Setting goals provides you with a clear roadmap for your business. Goals outline where you need to go and the steps to take along the way. They help focus your efforts in the right direction, ensuring that you work methodically toward achieving them. Without a clear goal, your efforts can easily become scattered, leading to wasted time and energy. Therefore, setting goals is vital for success, as it organizes your work and makes it more effective.

Real-Life Story: Ravi Chauhan, a young man from Delhi, began his network marketing journey but initially worked without setting clear goals. Every day, he met new people and tried to sell products, but he lacked direction. Eventually, his mentor advised him to set clear goals for his business. Ravi then set monthly targets, such as adding 10 new customers and 3 new team members. Once he started working toward these goals, his efforts became more focused, and he saw rapid growth. Within a few months, Ravi tripled the size of his team, and his income increased significantly.

Learning: Clear goals provide direction and ensure your efforts are purposeful. When you know where you're headed, every action you take moves you closer to success.

The SMART (Specific, Measurable, Achievable, Relevant, Time-bound) Goal System

Setting goals isn't just about having dreams—they need to be concrete and achievable. The SMART system helps make your goals clear and attainable.

- **Specific:** Your goal should be clear and specific. For example, instead of saying, "I want more clients," it's better to say, "I want to add 5 new clients this month."

- **Measurable:** Your goal should be something you can track. This helps you monitor your progress and stay on course.
- **Achievable:** Set goals that are realistic for you. If your goals are too high, you may feel discouraged.
- **Relevant:** Your goals should align with your larger objectives. Don't waste time on tasks that aren't directly related to your main goals.
- **Time-bound:** Each goal should have a specific timeframe, which adds discipline and structure to your efforts.

Real-Life Story: Neelam from Delhi, a successful network marketer, achieved great success by following the SMART system. She set a clear goal: "Add 20 new members to my team in 6 months." To ensure her goal was measurable, she aimed to add 3-4 new members each month. This goal was achievable based on her abilities and strategies. It was relevant because growing her team would expand her business. And finally, she set a deadline to achieve it within 6 months. Neelam accomplished her goal on time, thanks to the SMART approach.

Learning: The SMART system helps make your goals effective by creating a clear plan that you can measure and achieve. This clarity is crucial to success.

Short-Term and Long-Term Goals

To succeed in network marketing, you must set both short-term and long-term goals. Short-term goals are immediate targets, such as adding 5 new clients this month or recruiting 2 new team members. Long-term goals focus on your broader vision, like achieving a specific rank within a year or expanding your business internationally.

Real-Life Story: Sangeeta Sharma from Kanpur started her network marketing career without a long-term plan, which left her lacking direction. After some advice from her mentor, she set small short-term goals to build confidence. Her first goal was to acquire 5 new clients by the end of the month. When she accomplished this, her confidence grew, and she set a long-term goal to build a team of 100 people within a year. With these goals in place, Sangeeta gradually expanded her business, eventually becoming a leader of a large and successful team.

Learning: Short-term goals keep you motivated and build confidence, while long-term goals provide clarity and help you create a sustainable growth plan.

Measuring Your Progress Regularly

Once your goals are set, regularly measuring your progress is essential for success. Tracking your progress helps you see whether you are moving in the right direction or facing challenges. It enables you to understand what's working and where improvements are needed.

Here are some ways to measure progress effectively:

1. **Weekly Review:** Review your goals each week to assess your progress. This allows you to see if you're on track or need to work harder to meet your goals.
2. **Evaluation and Improvement:** If you find that you're not meeting your targets, adjust your strategy. Consider what changes or new approaches you can adopt.
3. **Sales and Network Data:** Regularly check your sales figures, new customer additions, and team expansion data. This provides a clear picture of how your business is progressing.

Measuring your progress keeps you on track and helps you identify areas where improvement is needed. Constant evaluation allows you to adjust your approach and ensures that you achieve your goals on time.

Real-Life Story: Vinay Jain from Raipur, a network marketer, set clear goals but failed to measure his progress regularly. He had no idea how close he was to achieving his targets or where he needed to improve. His mentor advised him to start tracking his progress weekly. After doing so, Vinay realized he wasn't getting the desired results in certain areas. Armed with this information, he refined his strategy and eventually began seeing significant improvement in his business.

Learning: Measuring progress is vital. It helps you understand if you're moving in the right direction and allows for timely adjustments to improve your chances of success.

Conclusion

Setting clear and achievable goals is a key factor in succeeding in network marketing. By using the SMART system, creating both short-term and long-term goals, and measuring your progress regularly, you increase your chances of success. Goals provide direction and motivation, and achieving them makes your progress tangible.

Remember, small goals and a big vision will make your path to success clear and achievable.

Reflective Questions for Personal and Business Growth

1. **Setting Goals:**
   - What short-term and long-term goals have you set for your business?
   - Are your goals aligned with the SMART system (Specific, Measurable, Achievable, Relevant, Time-bound)?
2. **SMART Goal System:**
   - Take one of your current goals and make it SMART—specific, measurable, achievable, relevant, and time-bound.
3. **Evaluating Progress:**
   - How has your progress been over the past month? Which goals did you accomplish, and which areas need improvement?
   - What tools or methods do you use to measure your progress?
4. **Regular Review and Improvement:**
   - Do you review your goals regularly? If not, when will you start?
   - If you are facing challenges, how will you improve your approach?

Final Message

"Goals are the direction that leads you to your dreams."

People like Ravi, Neelam, and Sangeeta achieved their success by setting clear goals and working hard to accomplish them. When you create specific and achievable goals, every step you take has meaning. Remember, small steps lead to big achievements. Set your goals, measure your progress, and strive to improve every day. Success will follow if you stay focused.

Your dreams are hidden in your goals. Take action today to make them a reality.

In network marketing, there's no need to worry when someone says 'no'. Every 'no' brings you closer to the person who will say 'yes'. Treat failure as a stepping stone to success because with each 'no', you learn and move closer to your goal. This is the journey to success.

7

Take Consistent Action

Success in network marketing doesn't happen overnight. It's a gradual process that requires consistent effort and patience. By taking small steps every day, you move steadily towards your goals. Consistency is the key to building momentum and achieving long-term success.

When you commit to doing something for your business daily—whether it's meeting potential clients, training your team, or expanding your knowledge—those small, consistent actions accumulate into big results over time. It's essential to stay persistent, even when progress seems slow. With consistent effort and regular action, you can build a stable and successful business.

The Importance of Consistency in Business

Consistent work keeps you disciplined and helps maintain stability in your business. It creates momentum and shows both your clients and team members that you are serious and fully dedicated to your work. This trust keeps people engaged with you and your business in the long run.

Consistency improves you day by day, bringing you closer to your goals. To achieve success, it's important to keep working regularly and remain patient.

Real-Life Story: Sumit Mishra, a young man from Lucknow, joined network marketing, but his start wasn't smooth. He worked hard initially but then stopped for a while, which caused his business to stagnate. Feeling discouraged, he sought advice from his mentor, who suggested that he should work a little every day, even if it was just a small task. Sumit took this advice seriously and started focusing on his business daily. Over time, his efforts paid off. Inspired by his consistency, Sumit's team also began working harder, and the business gradually improved.

Lesson: Consistency transforms your hard work into stability. It ensures that you keep moving toward your goals, and small steps taken regularly lead to long-term success.

Regular Time Management

Effective time management is critical for success in network marketing. Many people don't give regular time to their business, especially in the beginning, leading to disappointing results. However, when you schedule consistent time for your work, you will see progress more quickly.

For example, dedicating just one hour each day to your business can lead to significant progress over time. Proper time management brings discipline to your work and helps you reach your goals more efficiently.

Regularly setting aside time for your business channels your hard work in the right direction, increasing the likelihood of success.

Real-Life Story: Manju Mehta from Chandigarh was a housewife with family responsibilities but wanted to try her hand at network marketing. Initially, she struggled to find time, but soon she started setting aside two hours each day exclusively for her business. She used this time to meet new clients, follow up with potential leads, and interact with her team. With proper time management, her efforts paid off, and she became a successful network marketer, balancing both her business and family responsibilities.

Learning: Proper time management is key to success in network marketing. Dedicating a portion of your day to your business helps you reach your goals more quickly.

Focus on Key Activities

Not all tasks in network marketing contribute equally to your success. To grow your business efficiently, you need to focus on the activities that directly impact your success.

Prioritize meeting new potential clients, as this expands your network. Building and training your team is also crucial since it enables them to replicate your efforts. Additionally, following up with existing customers helps maintain strong relationships, increasing the likelihood of repeat business.

Invest your time and energy in tasks that directly contribute to the growth and success of your business for better and faster results.

Real-Life Story: Preeti Garg, a network marketer, was initially involved in many different tasks, from preparing presentations to posting on social media. Despite her efforts, she wasn't seeing the desired increase in her income. Her mentor advised her to focus on tasks that directly contribute to success—like meeting potential customers, motivating her team, and following up with clients. Preeti changed her strategy, focused on key activities, and soon saw her business improving. Her sales increased, and her team became more motivated.

Learning: To succeed in network marketing, focus on activities that directly impact your business. When you invest your time in the right areas, you will see more effective results.

How to Plan a Daily Routine

Establishing a consistent daily routine is crucial for becoming a successful network marketer. Planning your day in advance allows you to work in an organized and productive way. A structured routine keeps you disciplined and ensures that you are regularly moving toward your goals.

Here are some tips to create an effective daily routine:

- **Start Early:** Begin your day with positive thoughts and a simple plan. Identify the three major tasks you need to accomplish today to set your day off on the right path.
- **Prioritize Key Tasks:** Focus on the most important tasks first, such as contacting new potential clients or working with your team. This ensures that you concentrate on high-impact activities.
- **Schedule Follow-ups:** Set a specific time each day for following up with clients and team members. Regular follow-ups help maintain relationships and keep your business moving forward.
- **Meet New People:** Aim to meet or contact at least 1-2 new people each day. This helps you expand your network and grow your business consistently.

A well-planned routine will help you stay disciplined, making the path to success easier.

Real-Life Story: Rohit Sharma from Delhi initially struggled to organize his day when he started network marketing. Working without a plan slowed his progress. His mentor suggested creating a consistent daily routine. Rohit planned his day by dedicating an hour in the morning to contacting new leads, followed by an hour of follow-ups with existing clients, and then team meetings in the afternoon. This structured routine brought discipline to his work, and soon his business grew significantly.

Learning: A consistent routine keeps you disciplined and increases your chances of success. Planning your day regularly ensures you can work efficiently and effectively.

Conclusion

Consistent action is the foundation of success in network marketing. When you work on your business a little every day, those small steps accumulate into big results over time. By managing your time properly, focusing on key activities, and creating a consistent daily routine, you will steadily move toward your goals.

Remember, consistency is the key to success. Taking small steps daily will gradually pay off, leading you to a successful position in your network marketing business.

Reflective Questions for Personal and Business Growth

1. **Consistency Assessment:**
   - Are you working consistently on your business every day? If not, what small steps can you take to improve?

- How much time do you dedicate to your network marketing business each day?

2. **Time Management Review:**
   - Do you set aside a specific time each day for network marketing? If not, can you dedicate 1-2 hours?
   - What are the most important tasks of your day? Are you prioritizing them?
3. **Focus on Key Activities:**
   - Which tasks in your routine directly contribute to your business growth?
   - Are you focusing on key activities like meeting new clients, doing follow-ups, and communicating with your team?
4. **Daily Routine Planning:**
   - Do you start your day with a clear plan? If not, how can you improve your routine starting today?
   - What are the three key activities you plan to complete each day for your business?

Final Message

"Success belongs to those who take small, consistent steps daily."

People like Sumit, Manju, and Rohit have demonstrated that consistency and discipline are the true keys to success. When you take small, regular actions, they add up to significant results over time. Invest your time wisely, focus on the key activities, and establish a disciplined routine. Remember, every step brings you closer to your goal. Celebrate the small victories and enjoy the journey to success.

Your success is built on the consistent steps you take today—keep moving forward!

8

The Power of Duplication

One of the most important elements of success in network marketing is *duplication.* Duplication means sharing the strategies and methods you use with your team so they can replicate your success. When you create a strong system and implement it effectively within your team, the growth of your business multiplies. In this chapter, we will explore what duplication is, why it is crucial, and how you can implement it successfully in your network marketing business.

Importance of Duplication

Duplication in network marketing allows your team to adopt the same methods and strategies that have helped you grow your business. It's a process of sharing your experiences, methodologies, and successful techniques with team members, enabling them to replicate your success. The true power of duplication is that the business's growth no longer relies solely on your individual efforts—your entire team moves forward together. When you create a strong system and ensure your team follows it, the system becomes a guide for everyone, leading to exponential business growth.

Real-Life Story: Sanjay Chaudhary from Kanpur began his network marketing journey and achieved great success through hard work. However, he noticed that some of his team members were not as successful. Sanjay realized that if his team followed the same strategies he used, their results could improve. He shared his methods for meeting clients, conducting follow-ups, and building strong relationships. As his team members started replicating Sanjay's strategies, their success grew. Now, Sanjay's team is achieving great success together, and the business is growing rapidly.

Learning: Duplication means sharing your successful strategies with your team so that they can replicate your efforts. When the entire team works together, business growth multiplies.

Effective Training and System Building

Effective training and system building are vital for the success of your team in network marketing. This involves organizing your strategies and work methods in a way that your team can easily understand and implement. Start by breaking down your process into small, simple steps that even new members can follow. It's essential to train your team regularly, ensuring they continue to learn new skills and techniques. Personal guidance and support boost your team's confidence, helping them stay on track.

A clear and effective system allows your team to not only replicate your success but also improve upon it. This structure makes your team more organized and efficient, leading to faster business growth.

Real-Life Story: Nita Mehta from Bhopal built a large team through her hard work but noticed her team members weren't achieving the success they were capable of. To help them, Nita developed a training system. She began holding weekly training sessions, breaking down her successful techniques into short, simple steps. She also ensured that every team member had the necessary tools and guidance to follow the system. With this training system in place, her team's performance improved, and they started achieving greater success.

Learning: An effective system and regular training motivate your team to work in the right direction. When everyone follows the same system, the chances of success increase significantly.

Motivating Team Members to Duplicate

Motivation is a crucial aspect of duplication. Your team members will only replicate your methods when they see that your system works and brings success. It's essential to demonstrate that your approach is both simple and effective. When your team sees you succeeding using your strategies, they will be motivated to adopt the same methods. Your success and hard work will inspire them to follow your lead, leading to exponential growth for your team and business.

Real-Life Story: Aakash Ahuja from Raipur was a successful network marketer, but his team wasn't seeing the same level of success. He realized his team needed the right direction and motivation. Aakash spoke to his team individually, sharing his success stories and explaining how he achieved his results. He also conducted individual coaching sessions, where he guided them through his strategies. Gradually, Aakash's team started adopting his methods, and their success began to grow alongside his.

Learning: When you set an example and share your success stories, your team becomes inspired. This inspiration leads to team members replicating your strategies, which drives growth across the business.

Growing Your Business with the Power of Duplication

The biggest advantage of duplication is that it accelerates the growth of your business. When each team member works the same way you do, the results multiply, far exceeding what you could achieve alone. The larger your team, the more powerful the duplication process becomes.

Real-Life Story: Karan Pal from Meerut started slowly in network marketing but soon built a small team through steady effort. He realized that if his team adopted the same strategies he was using, they too could succeed more quickly. Karan taught his team the process of duplication, ensuring that every member followed the same steps for approaching clients, conducting follow-ups, and expanding the team. As his team began following this system, Karan's business grew rapidly. His team soon expanded across multiple states, and his income doubled.

Learning: Duplication is a powerful tool for exponential business growth. When your entire team follows a well-organized system, success comes faster, and the business becomes stronger and more sustainable.

Conclusion

The power of duplication is one of the greatest secrets to success in network marketing. By sharing your strategies and methods with your team and motivating them to follow your lead, your hard work is no longer just your own—it becomes a collective effort.

In this chapter, we explored how duplication works, why it's important, and how to apply it to your business. By building a strong system, training your team effectively, and keeping them motivated, you can fully harness the power of duplication to grow your business. Duplication is a transformative tool that can take your network marketing success to new heights.

Reflective Questions for Personal and Business Growth

1. **Start the Process of Duplication:**
   - Have you started the process of duplication in your business? If not, what strategies can you use to motivate your team to duplicate your methods?
   - Is your team able to understand and implement the system you've created?
2. **Effective Training and System Building:**
   - Do you have a consistent system that your team can easily follow and replicate?
   - What type of regular training program can you organize for your team?

3. **Motivating Team Members:**
   - ❍ Are you setting a strong example for your team to inspire them?
   - ❍ Are you regularly sharing your success stories and strategies with your team?
4. **Business Growth Plan:**
   - ❍ Have you developed a clear duplication plan for your team and business to grow quickly?
   - ❍ Are all your team members successfully adopting and implementing your system?

Final Message

"When you walk alone, you go fast, but when you walk with an organized team, you go far."

The power of duplication in network marketing is unparalleled. By sharing your strategies and experiences with your team, your success no longer depends solely on your efforts—it becomes a result of collective action.

Remember, with the right training, motivation, and an effective system, your team will move in the same direction, multiplying the business's success many times over. Duplication is the key to long-term growth and a sustainable, thriving business.

9

Importance of Follow-up

Follow-up is the foundation of success in network marketing. Whether you're dealing with a prospect or a team member, follow-up is the key that turns your efforts into results. Many people make initial contact but don't follow up, waiting for the other person to respond. However, without follow-up, you may miss out on the best opportunities to engage with your prospect or team member and bring them into your business.

In this chapter, we'll explore why follow-up is crucial, how to do it effectively, and how to strengthen relationships during the follow-up process.

The Right Time to Follow-up

The right time to follow up is after you've provided your prospect or team member with information and allowed them some time to consider it. Reaching out again at the right moment ensures that you remain in their thoughts and keeps your offer top of mind.

Real-Life Story: Rahul, a young network marketer, contacted many people initially but didn't follow up. When his mentor met with him, he advised Rahul that after making initial contact, it's essential to follow up. Rahul took this advice seriously and contacted the people he had spoken to earlier. Surprisingly, many of them were now interested after having some time to think. By following up at the right time, Rahul added several new clients and team members.

Learning: The first contact is important, but timely follow-up is what leads to success. Give people time to think, and then follow up to keep them engaged with your offer.

Regular Follow-up with Prospective Clients and Team Members

Regular follow-up is an effective way to grow your business steadily. One contact is not enough—you need to consistently reconnect with your prospects and team members to ensure they take your offer seriously.

Real-Life Story: Reema Patel, a network leader from Pune, initially contacted many potential customers, but none were interested in her products at first. Her mentor advised her not to get discouraged and to do regular follow-ups. Reema took this advice to heart and began contacting those prospects once a month, each time bringing new information—sometimes explaining the product's features, other times sharing company success stories. Over time, her persistence paid off, with people gradually showing interest in her products. This consistent follow-up led to increased sales and new members joining her team.

Lesson: Regular follow-up is essential in network marketing. Prospects may not be ready initially, but by staying in touch and providing new information, they are more likely to accept your offer when the time is right.

Building Rapport During Follow-up

Follow-up isn't just a formal process—it's an opportunity to strengthen relationships with your prospects and team members. When you follow up regularly, show that you care about more than just making a sale. Focus on understanding their needs and solving their problems, building trust and rapport.

Provide them with new information, help solve their issues, and always be ready to answer their questions. When customers or team members feel that you genuinely want to help, they will stay with you longer, which helps your business grow.

Real-Life Story: Aman Gupta, a network leader from Siliguri, was known for maintaining strong relationships with his customers. During follow-up, Aman wouldn't just talk about his products—he'd also ask about their personal lives, inquire about their families, and understand their needs. This personal attention created a deep bond between Aman and his customers. Whenever they needed a product, they would reach out to Aman first because they trusted him and knew he understood their needs.

Learning: When following up, don't just focus on making a sale—build a strong and trusting relationship with your customers. When people see you as a trusted advisor rather than just a salesperson, they are more likely to stay with you for the long term.

Organizing the Follow-up Process

To succeed with follow-up, it's important to have a systematic approach. Without a plan, you may lose track of potential clients and team members. Create a list with the names and contact details of the people you need to reconnect with and set reminders for follow-ups. A well-organized follow-up system ensures that you never miss an opportunity to strengthen relationships.

Real-Life Story: Kavita Biswas, a network leader from Kolkata, started with great enthusiasm but soon faced a challenge—she was unable to stay in regular touch with prospects and team members due to a lack of an organized follow-up process. Many times, she would forget to follow up on time, which negatively impacted her business. Her mentor advised her to use a CRM (Customer Relationship Management) tool to streamline her follow-up process. Kavita entered all her prospects' and team members' information into the tool and set reminders for when to follow up with each one. This system helped her stay on track, and the timely follow-ups strengthened her relationships, leading to rapid business growth.

Lesson: Organizing follow-up is essential. Whether you use CRM software or a simple notebook, an organized system can strengthen your relationships and keep your business on a stable and successful path.

Conclusion

Follow-up is invaluable in network marketing. Timely follow-up, regular contact, and building trusting relationships are key to moving your business forward. When you create meaningful connections with your customers and team members and keep your follow-up process organized, you increase your chances of success and establish long-term relationships.

Remember, follow-up isn't just about increasing sales—it's an opportunity to build a strong foundation for your business.

Reflective Questions for Personal and Business Growth

1. **Right Time to Follow-up:**
   - ❍ When was the last time you contacted a prospect or team member? Was it the right time to follow up?
   - ❍ Do you set a specific time frame for follow-up?
2. **Regular Follow-up:**
   - ❍ Do you regularly connect with your prospects and team members?
   - ❍ How many follow-ups do you aim to complete each month?
3. **Building Relationships:**
   - ❍ Do you try to build a personal connection with clients and team members when you follow up?
   - ❍ Do you keep personal information that can help strengthen your relationship with them?
3. **Streamlining the Follow-up Process:**
   - ❍ Do you have a system or tool to keep follow-up organized?
   - ❍ Do you follow up regularly to ensure you don't forget about any potential customers or team members?

Final Message

"Follow-up is the bridge that connects your efforts to success."

In network marketing, follow-up is one of the most important parts of your efforts. It's not just a reminder for your customers—it's a chance to build lasting relationships with them. Regular and organized follow-up not only grows your business but also demonstrates your dedication and seriousness toward your clients and team members.

Remember, timely follow-up not only opens the door to success but also lays the foundation for long-term relationships.

10

Building Relationships with Customers and Team Members

Network marketing isn't just about selling products—it's a business built on relationships. The foundation of your success lies in the connections you create with your customers and team members. When you establish deep, trusting relationships, your business extends beyond one-time sales, ensuring long-term success.

In this chapter, we'll explore the importance of long-term relationships, how to build trust with customers and team members, and how acting with honesty and transparency can strengthen your business.

The Importance of Long-Term Relationships

Building long-term relationships is essential for success in network marketing. When you nurture meaningful connections with your customers and team, they don't just become regular buyers—they also feel motivated to join and grow your business. These relationships are rooted in trust, which strengthens over time, providing stability for your business and empowering your team to perform better.

Real-Life Story: Neha Bansal from Saharanpur started her career in network marketing with a unique perspective. Instead of focusing solely on sales, she prioritized building personal relationships with her customers and team members. Neha believed that if she could connect deeply with her customers, they would not only become regular users of her products but also recommend her to others. She would talk to them regularly, ask about their families, and understand their needs. If a customer had a problem, Neha would find the right product or solution for them. This personal touch helped her build long-term relationships, resulting in steady business growth through referrals and customer loyalty.

Learning: Building long-term relationships is key to success in network marketing. When your customers trust you and feel connected, they become part of your business's growth and help it flourish.

How to Build Trusting Relationships with Customers and Team Members

Trust is the most important factor for success in network marketing. When customers and team members trust you, they're not just buying your products—they're listening to your advice and valuing your guidance. Trust is built gradually through honesty, transparency, and consistent support.

For customers, understanding their needs and recommending the right products builds trust. For team members, guiding them in the right direction, offering support, and staying connected strengthens their belief in you.

Real-Life Story: Atul Kamble from Pune realized early on that trust would be the driving force behind the success of his network marketing business. Atul took the time to have honest conversations with his clients, listening to their concerns and recommending suitable products. He also made personal connections with his team, helping them navigate their challenges and achieve their goals. As Atul's team saw that he genuinely cared about their success, their confidence grew, and they worked even harder.

Learning: Trust is the foundation of a successful and lasting business. When you act with honesty toward your clients and team, they will stay with you long-term and contribute to your success.

Working with Honesty and Transparency

Honesty and transparency are essential in network marketing. When you deal honestly with clients and team members, they begin to trust and remain loyal to you. Honesty means providing accurate information about your products, without exaggerating their benefits.

Transparency means sharing all necessary details about your business, whether it's product quality, commission structures, or business plans. When people see that you're being straightforward with them, their trust in you solidifies, and this trust spreads to both clients and team members. This leads to stronger, long-lasting relationships that provide stability to your business.

Real-Life Story: Sapna from Kolkata started in network marketing by always providing accurate information to her clients. If a product wasn't suitable for a client, she would honestly tell them and recommend a better option. Similarly, she always communicated openly with her team members about how to move forward in their business. Her honesty earned her respect from both clients and her team, and they followed her guidance, leading to rapid business growth.

Learning: Honesty and transparency are crucial for long-term success in network marketing. When your clients and team trust you, they will stay with you and support your business growth.

Understanding the Service and Needs of Customers

Network marketing is not just about selling products—it's a service-based business. You need to understand your customers' needs and provide them with the right solutions. When customers see that you care about their needs and offer thoughtful solutions, they view you as a trusted partner, not just a salesperson.

Offering solutions builds trust and loyalty, which strengthens your business in the long run. This service-oriented approach not only boosts sales but also establishes you as a respected network marketer.

Real-Life Story: Shyam Verma from Lucknow used a customer-focused approach to achieve success in network marketing. He personally spoke to each customer, listened to their problems, and suggested tailored solutions. His dedication to serving his customers made him extremely popular. Customers trusted him and referred him to their friends and family, which helped his business grow rapidly.

Learning: In network marketing, selling products isn't enough—understanding and addressing your customers' needs is essential. When you provide the right solutions, customers stay loyal and help grow your business.

Conclusion

Building strong relationships with customers and team members is the foundation of success in network marketing. Long-term relationships go beyond one-time sales and lead to lasting business growth.

When you build trust through honesty and transparency, and when you understand and address the needs of your customers and team, you create a loyal network that supports and contributes to your success.

By focusing on relationships, you can build a sustainable and thriving network marketing business.

Reflective Questions for Personal and Business Growth

1. **Long-term Relationships:**
   - ❍ Are you focused on building long-term relationships with your customers and team members?
   - ❍ How do you ensure your relationships go beyond one-time sales?
2. **Trust Building:**
   - ❍ Do your customers and team members trust you? How do you know?
   - ❍ What steps can you take to build more trust in your business?
3. **Honesty and Transparency:**
   - ❍ Do you share information about your products and business with complete honesty?

- ❍ Are you maintaining transparency with your customers and team members?

4. **Customer Service:**
   - ❍ Do you make an effort to understand the needs of your customers?
   - ❍ Have you recently gone the extra mile to solve a customer's problem?

Final Message

"The road to success in network marketing is built on the foundation of relationships."

Relationships aren't just a part of the business—they *are* the business. When you build strong, trusting relationships with your customers and team members, your business doesn't stop at one-time sales—it moves toward long-term success.

Remember, true success comes when you see your customers and team members as partners in your journey, building connections based on trust and service rather than just profit.

11

Importance of Teamwork

Teamwork is an essential component of success in network marketing. Your team is your greatest asset, and when all team members work together, your business can grow exponentially. However, teamwork is not just about dividing tasks—it's about fostering trust, cooperation, and mutual growth.

In this chapter, we will explore the importance of teamwork, how to build trust and cooperation within your team, and strategies to keep the team motivated and active. Additionally, we'll learn from real-life examples of individuals who have achieved success through teamwork.

Building Cooperation and Trust Within the Team

Cooperation and trust are the cornerstones of effective teamwork. When team members collaborate and trust each other, the quality and speed of their work improve. Cooperation allows large tasks to be broken down into manageable pieces, making them easier to complete. Moreover, when team members trust each other, morale increases, and they are more likely to share ideas openly.

In a positive and supportive environment, each member understands their responsibilities and works with full dedication. This collective improvement leads to enhanced team performance and business growth.

By fostering cooperation and trust, you amplify the strength of your team, leading to faster and more sustainable success.

Real-Life Story: Sandeep from Raipur, a network marketing leader, had a large team, but there was a lack of coordination among the members. No one was working well with each other, which impacted the team's overall performance. Recognizing this issue, Sandeep decided to build an environment of cooperation and trust. He organized a group workshop where team members could share their challenges and concerns openly.

As members listened to each other, they began to understand each other's problems better and found new ways to help. This created a sense of collaboration within the team, and gradually, trust developed. The team started performing better both individually and collectively, and they began reaching new goals together.

Learning: Cooperation and trust are crucial for successful teamwork. When team members support each other and work with trust, the business's success grows exponentially.

Leadership Development and Team Building

Leadership plays a vital role in teamwork. A good leader provides direction and makes the path to success clearer and easier. Without strong leadership, teams may lack unity and coordination, leading to suboptimal results.

A leader's responsibility is not only to guide the team but also to inspire others to become leaders themselves. When every member of the team starts taking responsibility and sees themselves as a leader, the entire team becomes more motivated, cooperative, and effective. Leadership fosters confidence and a sense of responsibility, ensuring collective progress.

Real-Life Story: Rajni Bala from Jaipur had a great start in network marketing but soon realized her team needed stronger leadership to move forward. To address this, she assigned small leadership tasks to each member of her team. Some members were responsible for organizing team meetings, others guided new members, and a few were in charge of training sessions.

This strategy increased the confidence of all team members, as they began taking ownership of their tasks. Over time, each member developed leadership qualities, which united the team and improved their overall performance.

Learning: Developing leadership within the team is essential for success. When every member is given the opportunity to lead, their sense of responsibility increases, and the team's performance improves. A good leader nurtures these qualities in their team to achieve collective success.

Celebrating Team Achievements

Recognizing and celebrating achievements is an important aspect of teamwork. When you acknowledge and celebrate the small and big successes of your team, it boosts their morale. Each member feels valued, and this recognition motivates them to work harder towards future goals.

Celebrating achievements creates a positive atmosphere within the team, promoting unity and encouraging everyone to strive for even greater success.

Real-Life Story: Dinesh Bansal from Saharanpur, a network leader, noticed that while his team achieved several small goals each month, he had only been celebrating the bigger wins. Realizing the importance of recognizing every success, Dinesh decided to highlight and celebrate the smaller achievements during team meetings. He praised each member's hard work, which made them feel valued and appreciated. As a result, team members were more motivated and began working with renewed enthusiasm.

Learning: Celebrating small achievements keeps morale high and reinforces the importance of every member's contribution. This fosters a positive and productive team culture, enhancing the chances of future success.

Keeping the Team Motivated and Energized

As a leader, one of your most important responsibilities is to keep your team motivated and energized. When enthusiasm wanes, it directly impacts the progress of the business. It's essential to continually implement new methods and strategies to keep your team motivated and focused.

For example, regular meetings where team members can share challenges and successes, setting clear targets, and offering rewards for performance can keep the team's energy high. Recognizing and celebrating even small efforts can boost morale and keep the team engaged.

Real-Life Story: Priya Bansal from Saharanpur noticed that her team's enthusiasm, which was high initially, had started to wane. To reignite their motivation, she introduced new strategies. Priya organized competitions within the team, offering prizes for the highest sales or the most new members added. This sparked a spirit of friendly competition, re-energizing the team. She also set monthly targets and shared personal success stories to inspire and motivate the team.

Over time, Priya's team regained their momentum, and the members started working with renewed energy and focus.

Learning: To keep the team motivated, leaders must introduce new goals, competitions, and motivational stories. This ensures that team members stay active, engaged, and focused on business growth.

Conclusion

Teamwork is essential for success in network marketing. When your team works together, your business progresses faster and more effectively.

Fostering cooperation and trust, developing leadership within the team, celebrating achievements, and keeping the team motivated are the hallmarks of a strong and successful team. When your team works in harmony, you don't just reach your goals—you achieve success together.

The power of teamwork can take your business to new heights. Maintain collaboration, motivation, and support within your team, and you'll be well on your way to success.

Reflective Questions for Personal and Business Growth

1. **Collaboration and Trust:**
   - Are you creating an environment of collaboration and trust within your team?
   - What steps can you take to improve collaboration among your team members?

2. **Leadership Development:**
    - Are you providing leadership opportunities to your team members?
    - How can you encourage other team members to develop leadership qualities?
3. **Celebrating Achievements:**
    - Do you recognize and celebrate both small and large achievements within your team?
    - How can you celebrate team achievements to boost motivation?
4. **Keeping the Team Motivated:**
    - Do you regularly adopt new strategies to keep your team motivated?
    - What new initiatives or contests can you introduce to keep your team active and energized?

Final Message

"Success is not a solo journey—it is the achievement of a united team."

Your team is your greatest strength in network marketing. When you work together, trust each other, and maintain collaboration, your business will progress more rapidly.

Remember, you can run fast alone, but with a strong team, you will go far.

12

Effective Use of Online Tools and Social Media

In today's digital age, network marketing has evolved in a way that makes growing your business easier and faster than ever before. While traditional methods required time-consuming face-to-face meetings, platforms like Facebook, Instagram, WhatsApp, and LinkedIn now allow you to connect with thousands of people and share information about your products and services instantly. Digital marketing strategies—such as posts, videos, and webinars—not only help you reach more people but also save time and money. By using the right online strategies, you can accelerate the growth of your business and achieve long-term success.

In this chapter, we'll explore how to use online tools and social media effectively to grow your network marketing business. Additionally, we'll share real-life stories of individuals who have successfully harnessed these tools to achieve success.

Network Marketing Strategies in the Digital Age

The digital age has transformed network marketing, making it more accessible than ever. You no longer need to travel long distances or invest hours in in-person meetings to build relationships. With the right use of digital tools, you can connect with potential customers and team members from anywhere at any time, taking your business beyond geographical boundaries.

Real-Life Story: Nisha Sharma initially felt confined to working within her locality after starting her network marketing journey. Her mentor encouraged her to expand her business using social media and digital tools. Nisha started being active on platforms like Facebook and Instagram, regularly posting about her products and services while reaching out to potential customers. Over time, she built a thriving digital network that extended far beyond her local area, even reaching cities and regions she had never considered before. As a result, her business grew rapidly, thanks to her digital strategies.

Learning: In today's digital age, social media and online tools are crucial for network marketing success. They allow you to break through local limitations, connect with a larger audience, and grow your business faster.

Effective Use of Social Media Platforms

Social media is one of the most powerful tools for network marketing today. Platforms like Facebook, Instagram, and LinkedIn offer the opportunity to connect with people globally without physical limitations. Your regular activity on these platforms significantly impacts your success. By adopting the right strategies, you can easily reach new potential customers, introduce them to your products, and even build your team.

Effective Use of Online Tools...

Sharing success stories, showcasing product features, and posting valuable content can help you expand your audience and grow your business.

Real-Life Story: Aditya Kumar leveraged social media to fast-track the growth of his network marketing business. He created professional profiles on Facebook and Instagram, consistently posting valuable content. Aditya shared customer success stories, provided simple and effective product usage tips, and delivered key business insights. These posts helped him grow his follower base and attract new customers and team members. Within a few months, Aditya connected with hundreds of new potential customers, expanding his business rapidly and strengthening his digital presence.

Learning: Consistent activity on social media, paired with the right content and engagement strategies, can significantly grow your network marketing business. Posting regularly and engaging effectively helps you reach a wider audience and attract customers.

The Right Use of CRM and Email Marketing Tools

Using CRM (Customer Relationship Management) and email marketing tools efficiently is a key factor in network marketing success. CRM tools allow you to organize customer information, preferences, purchase history, and other key details, making it easier to follow up at the right time and meet customer needs effectively.

Email marketing tools enable you to send regular updates, promotions, and important information to your customers and team members. These tools help you stay connected and inform customers about new products and services. The proper use of CRM and email marketing tools can help you build long-term relationships and promote your business effectively.

Real-Life Story: Vinod Prasad from Ratlam, Madhya Pradesh, started using a CRM system to organize his network marketing business. Initially, Vinod kept customer and team member information on paper or in mobile notes, which made it difficult to track follow-ups and stay organized. After adopting a CRM tool, Vinod could store all relevant information systematically. He then began sending regular email updates to his contacts, keeping them informed about new products and services. This organized approach improved his customer relationships and follow-up efficiency, leading to increased sales and business growth.

Learning: Using CRM and email marketing tools effectively can make your business more organized and efficient. These tools help manage contacts, provide timely follow-ups, and ensure consistent communication, all of which are critical for success.

The Power of Virtual Meetings and Webinars

Virtual meetings and webinars have revolutionized network marketing, making it easier to connect with prospects and team members from anywhere. Platforms like Zoom, Google Meet, and Microsoft Teams allow you to conduct virtual presentations and training sessions, saving time while expanding your reach.

With virtual meetings, you can easily share business presentations, showcase products and services, and train your team. Virtual platforms make it possible to connect with more people in less time, taking network marketing to a new level of efficiency.

Real-Life Story: Vikas Kataria from Bhagalpur, Bihar, found it challenging to meet all his potential clients and team members in person due to the large number of people he was managing. To overcome this, Vikas started using virtual meeting platforms like Zoom and conducted weekly webinars. These webinars allowed him to share business information, answer questions, and showcase new products. Vikas saved time and was able to connect with far more people, significantly growing his team and business. His virtual presence became a key driver of his success.

Learning: Virtual meetings and webinars offer an effective way to connect with more people while saving time. They make your business more efficient and scalable.

Conclusion

In today's digital age, online tools and social media have transformed the way network marketing works. By leveraging the right digital tools, you can expand your business beyond geographical limitations and achieve success faster. Effective use of social media, CRM, email marketing tools, and virtual platforms can take your network marketing business to new heights.

The proper use of digital tools not only saves time but also helps you build lasting relationships with clients and team members.

Reflective Questions for Personal and Business Growth

1. **Use of Online Tools:**
   - Are you using digital tools (CRM, email marketing, social media) in your business?

- If not, what online tools can you start using to improve your business?

2. **Social Media Presence:**
   - Do you regularly share content related to your business on Facebook, Instagram, or LinkedIn?
   - What is your current social media strategy, and how can you make it more effective?
3. **Virtual Meetings and Webinars:**
   - Do you hold virtual meetings or webinars?
   - What types of virtual events can you add to your business that would benefit your clients and team?
4. **Use of CRM and Email Marketing:**
   - Have you set up CRM or email marketing tools for your clients and team?
   - How can you use these tools to make your business more organized and efficient?

Final Message

"In the digital age, the limits of your success are only limited by your imagination."

Online tools and social media have taken network marketing to a new level. With the right digital platforms and strategies, you can access opportunities that were once out of reach. Strengthen your online presence, adopt digital strategies, and take your business to new heights.

13

Self-Motivation and Self-Discipline

The key to success in network marketing is self-motivation and self-discipline. In this business, you are your own biggest partner. You must constantly keep yourself motivated towards your goals and manage your activities with discipline. The better you manage your time and tasks, the faster you'll progress towards success. In this chapter, we will discuss the importance of self-discipline, how to stay motivated, and the dedication required for personal growth.

Importance of Self-Discipline in Network Marketing

Self-discipline is crucial in network marketing because you are your own boss. There is no one to tell you when or how to work, so your success depends entirely on how disciplined you are. Self-discipline is the force that drives you toward your goals day after day.

In network marketing, you have to decide for yourself when to hold meetings, when to contact clients, and when to meet potential customers. If you work with discipline, you can conduct timely follow-ups and keep your business moving forward. Self-discipline is the foundation of success that keeps you consistent and dedicated.

Real-Life Story: *Satish Deshmukh from Kolhapur, Maharashtra, faced significant challenges when he started network marketing. The first few months were tough, and he struggled to manage his activities, which slowed his progress. He felt lost about how to move his business forward.*

A mentor advised Satish to adopt self-discipline. Following his mentor's suggestion, Satish began making daily task lists and committed to completing every task on time. He learned to manage his time better and set his priorities correctly.

Within a few months, Satish's hard work and self-discipline led him to success. His team grew rapidly, and his network marketing business flourished.

Learning: Without self-discipline, it is hard to achieve continuous progress in network marketing. Staying disciplined with your time and tasks is the foundation that will drive your business to new heights over the long term.

How to Keep Yourself Motivated

In network marketing, staying motivated every day is essential for success. This is a business that demands constant effort, and at times, you may face rejection that can lower your morale. But the real challenge is how to keep yourself motivated. Focusing on your goals and tracking your progress daily will help you stay motivated. Setting small, achievable goals can also provide a source of encouragement.

Self-motivation is the strength that helps you overcome obstacles and move forward. With this inner drive, you can continuously pursue success in your network marketing business.

Real-Life Story: *Suman Kashyap from Rohtak, Haryana, faced many rejections when she first started network marketing. It was a frustrating time, but she refused to give up. During these tough moments, Suman focused on her dreams to keep herself motivated. Each morning, she would ask herself, "Why am I doing this?" This thought reignited her energy each day.*

Suman also began reading inspirational books and stories about network marketing success, which helped her maintain a positive mindset. Hearing the success stories of others reminded her that failure is just a step along the way to success, and persistent efforts are necessary.

These habits kept Suman motivated every day. She did not allow failure to dominate her, and she faced every challenge head-on. Eventually, her hard work and self-motivation led to success.

Learning: Remembering your goals, reading motivational books, and learning from the stories of others are key ways to stay motivated. Self-motivation is the tool that gives you the courage to keep moving forward in the face of struggles.

Time Management and Prioritization

Effective time management is critical for success in network marketing. When you manage your time well and prioritize tasks, you can achieve more in less time. Network marketers often juggle meeting clients, training teams, and contacting potential customers. By planning your day in advance and prioritizing tasks, you make your workload more manageable.

Good time management not only boosts productivity but also creates a sense of balance and organization. Making steady progress every day brings you closer to your goals. Proper time management enables you to be more effective and achieve success faster in your network marketing business.

Real-Life Story: *Neelam Agarwal from Surat, Gujarat, struggled with managing her time when she started network marketing. She found it difficult to balance her business and personal life, and the mounting workload caused her stress. Determined to take control, she focused on improving her time management skills.*

Neelam created a daily schedule, prioritizing the most important tasks. She completed key business activities—such as contacting clients, training team members, and reaching out to new prospects—early in the day. Afterward, she focused on personal tasks.

With proper planning, Neelam found she could accomplish more in less time. As her time management skills improved, so did her business. Neelam now feels more balanced and organized, and her business continues to grow.

Learning: Time management allows you to conduct your day more effectively. Prioritize your most important tasks and make the best use of your time. This will help your business grow faster and make you more successful.

Self-Motivation and Self-Discipline

Dedication to Personal Development

To succeed in network marketing, it's crucial to invest in your personal development. This business isn't just about selling products or building connections—it's also a journey of personal growth. As you improve your skills and knowledge, you'll become better equipped to connect with customers and lead your team. Qualities like confidence, communication skills, and leadership are essential for becoming a successful network marketer.

When you invest in personal growth, it positively impacts your business. Your improvements also inspire your team to do their best. Therefore, success in network marketing requires dedication not only to your business but also to your personal development. As you grow, so does your business.

Real-Life Story: Amit Bhatt from Jammu and Kashmir spent several years in network marketing but experienced real success only when he focused on his personal development. Previously, Amit concentrated solely on selling products and recruiting people. However, he realized that wasn't enough.

Amit began reading books on network marketing and motivation, attending seminars, and developing his leadership skills. He understood that self-improvement would allow him to guide his team more effectively. As Amit's confidence and communication skills improved, his team began to grow faster. This focus on personal development contributed significantly to his business's success, and his team members were inspired by his hard work and discipline.

Learning: To succeed in network marketing, focus on personal development. When you improve yourself, your business grows, and your team is inspired by your example.

Conclusion

Self-motivation and self-discipline are the cornerstones of success in network marketing. By keeping yourself motivated, practicing self-discipline, and managing your time effectively, you can overcome any challenge. Dedication to personal growth will not only enhance your skills but also help your business reach new heights.

Believe in yourself, keep learning, and use your time wisely. These principles will help you become a successful network marketer.

Reflective Questions for Personal and Business Growth

1. **Self-Discipline:**
   - Have you created a regular timetable for your daily tasks?
   - How can you discipline your actions further to stay consistent?
2. **Self-Motivation:**
   - Do you remind yourself of your goals daily to stay motivated?
   - What steps can you take to maintain your motivation?
3. **Time Management and Prioritization:**
   - Are you prioritizing your most important tasks?
   - What changes can you make to manage your time better?

4. Personal Development:

- Do you regularly focus on personal development (e.g., reading books, attending seminars)?
- What new steps can you take to improve your skills?

Final Message

"You are your biggest companion on the path to success."

Self-motivation and self-discipline are the forces that empower you to overcome every challenge. When you stay motivated, practice discipline, and pursue continuous personal growth, success is inevitable.

Believe in yourself, take consistent action, and success will be yours.

In network marketing, the relationships you build are your greatest strength. The better you connect with people and foster trust, the more successful you will become. Strong relationships pave the way to success because people trust you and are more willing to support you.

14

Facing Challenges and Learning From Them

The road to success in network marketing is not without obstacles. Every day may bring new challenges, such as rejection, market competition, or personal difficulties. However, true success is achieved by those who confront these challenges with a positive attitude. When you see challenges as opportunities and learn from them, you set yourself on the path to growth. Instead of seeing rejection as a setback, view it as a chance to improve and learn from your experiences.

Those who master the art of turning challenges into opportunities can go far in network marketing. This business is a journey of continuous learning and improvement, and success comes from facing challenges and moving forward.

In this chapter, we'll explore how to handle rejection, navigate competition, overcome personal and professional challenges, and turn difficulties into opportunities. We'll also look at real-life stories of individuals who have succeeded by adopting these principles.

Accepting Rejection and Learning From It

Rejection is one of the biggest challenges in network marketing. People may say "no" to your offers, and that's completely normal. When presenting your products or business, not everyone will say "yes" right away. The key is how you handle rejection. Instead of taking it personally, see it as a learning opportunity. Every "no" is a chance to improve, to reassess your approach, or to understand that the person may not be ready at the moment.

Rejection is part of the journey toward success in network marketing. Those who approach it with a positive mindset ultimately succeed. Rejection makes you stronger and prepares you for future challenges. Remember, every "no" brings you closer to a "yes." With this attitude, you can thrive in network marketing.

Real-Life Story: Anuj Malhotra from Delhi started network marketing with great enthusiasm. Initially, he was full of hope, but soon faced rejection. People weren't interested in what he had to offer, and this discouraged him. However, instead of giving up, Anuj saw rejection as a chance to learn. He realized there was a reason behind every "no" and began focusing on improving his approach. He changed his presentation style and learned to understand his prospects' needs and problems better. Instead of just pushing his products, he started explaining how his products could solve people's issues.

Gradually, his strategy worked. The number of rejections decreased, and he was able to connect with more people. Anuj discovered that rejection is simply part of the process and shouldn't be taken personally.

Learning: Treat rejection as a learning opportunity, not a defeat. Each "no" gives you a chance to correct your approach and get closer to a "yes." Success in network marketing comes from patience, a willingness to learn, and continuous effort.

Dealing with Market Competition

Market competition is a constant in network marketing. Many people sell the same or similar products and services, so you may find yourself needing to prove the value of what you offer. However, competition shouldn't discourage you. With the right strategies and a positive attitude, you can thrive in a competitive environment. Start by understanding your product's unique qualities and how it meets customer needs. When you demonstrate how your product can solve problems, people will be more likely to choose you.

Stay informed about market trends and competitors' activities. Continuously improve your marketing and sales techniques. With a positive mindset and a clear plan, you can overcome competition and succeed in your network marketing business.

Real-Life Story: Vaishali Khade from Mumbai faced significant competition when she started network marketing. Many others were selling the same product, making it hard for her to stand out. But instead of being intimidated by the competition, Vaishali focused on her unique strengths. She realized that success required something different. Vaishali began building strong relationships with her customers and offering exceptional customer service. She took the time to understand each customer's needs and provided tailored solutions, earning their trust.

Her honesty and dedication set her apart from the crowd. Gradually, customers began to prefer Vaishali's service, and her team grew rapidly. Her commitment and hard work allowed her to rise above the competition.

Learning: Don't fear competition—focus on your unique selling proposition (USP). Build strong relationships with customers and offer them added value. Competition is an opportunity to improve, so keep refining your approach to stand out.

Solving Personal and Professional Challenges

In network marketing, you may encounter challenges when family or friends don't take your business seriously, leading to disappointment. This is normal, but it's crucial to stay focused and confident in your goals. Use rejection as a learning opportunity to strengthen your resolve.

Time management is another significant challenge. Balancing personal and professional life requires setting priorities and allocating time wisely. Additionally, building and motivating a team can be difficult. Maintaining regular communication and offering support is key to overcoming these challenges.

Providing honest information and ensuring customer satisfaction are essential for success. By facing these obstacles with patience and a well-thought-out plan, you can achieve success in your network marketing business.

Real-Life Story: Deepak Batra from Banaras faced skepticism from family and friends when he started network marketing.

They doubted whether this business could bring him success. Initially, this discouraged Deepak, but instead of giving up, he remained focused on his plan.

Deepak improved his time management skills and developed a strategy that allowed him to balance both family and business. He consistently organized his work and concentrated on growing his business through hard work. Over time, his efforts paid off, and he began to succeed.

As Deepak's success grew, the attitude of his family and friends changed. Those who once doubted him began to praise and support him fully.

Learning: Patience and time management are crucial when facing personal and professional challenges. Stick to your plan, and don't let negativity bring you down. Use criticism as motivation to keep pushing forward.

Turning Challenges into Opportunities

The art of turning challenges into opportunities lies in viewing difficulties and rejections as learning moments. When faced with rejection, take it positively and assess what you can improve. This mindset allows you to learn from each difficult situation and grow. By maintaining confidence, patience, and a positive attitude, you can enjoy small successes while continuing to work toward larger goals. View failure as temporary, and find the hidden opportunities within each setback. This way, every challenge becomes a part of your growth and leads you toward success.

*Real-Life Story***:** Megha Patkar from Nashik faced a major setback when several key team members left her network marketing business. This was a significant challenge, as her team's strength suddenly weakened, and her business was affected. However, instead of giving up, Megha saw this difficulty as a new opportunity.

She focused on recruiting new team members and used this time to further develop her leadership skills. Megha worked closely with her new team, training and motivating them. In the process, she not only rebuilt her team but also became a stronger leader. Within months, her new team was more robust than before, and her business began to grow rapidly again.

Learning: Turn challenges into opportunities. Every difficult situation makes you stronger. This positive attitude is key to achieving success.

Conclusion

Challenges are an integral part of network marketing, but success comes to those who approach them with the right attitude and learn from them. Whether dealing with rejection, navigating competition, overcoming personal and professional difficulties, or transforming challenges into opportunities, these strategies will help you become a successful network marketer.

Remember, challenges are stepping stones to success. By facing them head-on, you not only take a step forward but also cross important milestones on your journey to success.

Reflective Questions for Personal and Business Growth

1. **Accept Rejection and Learn:**
   - Are you learning something from every rejection?
   - The next time you hear a "no," what strategy will you use?

2. **Deal with Competition:**
   - Have you added unique value to your business that sets you apart from the competition?
   - What additional benefits can you offer your customers?
3. **Address Personal and Professional Challenges:**
   - Have you created a time management plan to balance personal and professional responsibilities?
   - How can you gain positive support from your family and friends?
4. **Turn Challenges into Opportunities:**
   - How can you turn your recent challenge into an opportunity?
   - The next time you face difficulty, how will you maintain a positive attitude?

Final Message

"Challenges make us stronger, and rejection is the first step to success."

The road to success in network marketing may be tough, but those who face challenges with a positive mindset will ultimately succeed. View every challenge as an opportunity, and write your success story by overcoming each one.

Your success in network marketing is determined by how much you help others and how much value you place on them. When you understand the needs of your team and customers and prioritize their well-being, they begin to trust you. This trust becomes the key driver of your success.

15

Leadership and Motivation

Leadership and motivation are the driving forces that can elevate your success in network marketing. To be an effective leader, it is crucial not only to guide your team but also to keep them motivated and supported. In network marketing, leadership goes beyond giving orders—it's about motivating, supporting, and working alongside others. In this chapter, we will explore how to become an effective leader, develop leadership qualities within your team, and maintain team motivation and support. We'll also look at real-life stories of individuals who have used these principles to achieve success.

How to Be an Effective Leader in Network Marketing

A good leader is characterized by their honesty, decision-making abilities, and commitment to their team. A leader listens to their team members, understands their challenges, and guides them in the right direction. Effective leaders motivate their teams and support their growth. To keep the team unified, it is essential to foster trust, cooperation, and open communication. When team members trust each other and work collaboratively, they deliver better results. Strong leadership ensures that the team stays focused and moves in the right direction.

Being an effective leader in network marketing means guiding your team to success while working alongside them. A good leader understands the needs of the team, provides motivation, and helps solve problems.

Real-Life Story: Rajesh was working with a network marketing company, but his team's progress was slow. He realized that setting goals alone wouldn't work—his team also needed motivation and support. Rajesh started speaking with each team member individually, understanding their concerns, and offering tailored guidance for their development. Gradually, his team's performance improved, and they began achieving remarkable success.

Lesson: An effective leader works closely with their team, listens to their challenges, and provides support and motivation. When you bring your team along with you, success is inevitable.

Developing Leadership Qualities Within the Team

To build a strong and successful team, it is essential to foster leadership qualities in your team members. When team members begin taking on leadership responsibilities, the team grows rapidly and moves toward success.

Real-Life Story: Manju Sharma from Bhubaneswar led a network marketing team but was dissatisfied with their performance. Upon reflection, she realized the team lacked leadership qualities. Team members were hesitant to make decisions and unable to resolve challenges independently. Manju decided to focus on developing leadership within her team. She taught them how to make decisions, solve problems, and lead smaller teams. She encouraged them to take responsibility and work independently. Over time, her team members began taking on leadership roles, becoming more confident in their decision-making. This not only relieved Manju's workload but also improved the team's performance. As a result, her business experienced rapid growth.

Learning: Developing leadership qualities within the team is crucial. When team members start taking responsibility, the team becomes more effective and moves toward success more quickly.

Motivating and Supporting Team Members

Effective leaders know how to handle conflicts within the team to ensure business growth is not hindered. Understanding the root cause of the problem is the first step. Listening to all parties calmly and impartially is critical for making fair decisions. Fostering a sense of mutual respect and cooperation within the team strengthens relationships, leading to better collaboration. Regular meetings and open communication help clear misunderstandings and keep everyone aligned. A positive and supportive environment ensures that the team works together harmoniously, contributing to the overall success of the business.

Keeping your team motivated and supported is a hallmark of a successful leader. A motivated team can achieve even the most challenging goals. Therefore, it is essential to continually encourage your team and provide support when needed.

Real-Life Story: Nitin Kapoor from Amritsar started well with his network marketing team, but over time, his team became disheartened and unmotivated. Nitin realized that his team needed fresh motivation to work with the same enthusiasm they had initially. He began holding regular meetings to discuss progress, solve challenges, and offer motivation. Nitin celebrated even small achievements within the team, fostering a positive atmosphere. Whether it was meeting a minor goal or overcoming a challenge, Nitin and his team embraced every success together. His support and motivation reignited the team's energy, leading to significant improvements in performance.

Learning: A motivated and supported team consistently delivers better results. Celebrating small victories and maintaining regular communication keeps the team's energy high, helping them achieve long-term success.

Skills and Qualities Required for Leadership

To become an effective leader, you must develop several key qualities. First and foremost is the ability to listen—this allows you to understand your team's needs and concerns. Communication skills are also crucial, enabling you to convey your ideas clearly and motivate your team effectively.

Decision-making is another critical skill; a leader must be able to make the right decisions at the right time. Problem-solving skills are equally important, as they enable you to help your team navigate challenges.

Patience and dedication are essential when guiding your team. By creating an environment of cooperation and trust, you allow team members to work together productively. When a leader develops these skills, they not only achieve personal success but also lead their team to success.

Real-Life Story: Rakesh Kumar from Patna, Bihar, experienced early success in network marketing. However, as his team grew, he realized that selling products alone wasn't enough. He needed to become a true leader for his team.

Rakesh first developed his listening skills, paying close attention to each team member's concerns. He also honed his problem-solving abilities, helping the team tackle challenges with patience and guidance. Over time, his leadership strengthened his team, and today he is regarded as a successful network marketing leader. His team members appreciate his support and leadership.

Learning: Patience, problem-solving, and listening skills are critical for effective leadership. When you develop these abilities, you not only improve your team's performance but also become a better leader.

Conclusion

In network marketing, the balance between leadership and motivation is key to success. To be an effective leader, you must inspire and guide your team members, helping them develop their own leadership qualities. By keeping your team motivated and adopting the necessary leadership skills, you can build a strong and successful business.

Remember, a great leader doesn't just seek success for themselves—they guide and support their team toward collective success. When you become a true leader, both your team and your business will reach new heights.

Reflective Questions for Personal and Business Growth

1. **Leadership Development:**
   - ❍ Do you listen carefully to your team members' challenges?
   - ❍ Have you created a personal development plan for each team member?
2. **Maintaining Motivation:**
   - ❍ How do you regularly motivate your team members?
   - ❍ Do you celebrate your team's achievements and encourage them?
3. **Developing Leadership Qualities in the Team:**
   - ❍ Do you give your team members opportunities to lead?
   - ❍ Have you assigned small leadership tasks to help them take responsibility?
4. **Improving Leadership Skills:**
   - ❍ Are you actively developing your listening and problem-solving skills?
   - ❍ Do you approach your team's challenges with calmness and patience?

Final Message

"True leaders are those who pave the way for success not only for themselves but for their entire team."

Your team is your greatest strength in network marketing. As an effective leader, it is your responsibility to keep them motivated, supported, and guided in the right direction. When you embrace the role of a true leader, your team and your business will soar to new heights of success.

16

Ethics and Honesty in Network Marketing

Ethics and honesty are vital in network marketing. These principles not only help build trust, but also lead to long-term success. Ethical business practices increase your credibility and foster strong relationships with customers and team members, laying the foundation for sustained growth.

In this chapter, we will explore the importance of ethics in network marketing, how to build a business with integrity, and why adhering to ethical practices is essential for long-term success. We will also share real-life stories of individuals who achieved success by following ethical principles.

The Importance of Ethical Business Practices

Ethical business practices are the cornerstone of success in network marketing. When you operate with honesty, customers and team members develop trust in you, leading to long-term loyalty. Ethical practices involve sharing accurate information, avoiding deception, and maintaining honesty in all situations.

By working ethically, you strengthen your reputation and bring stability to your business. People prefer to work with individuals they trust. When ethics are at the core of your business, success is more likely. Trust is the foundation of any long-lasting network marketing venture, and following the right path helps to build that trust with both customers and team members.

Real-Life Story: Suresh Tiwari from Patna, Bihar, entered network marketing with deep knowledge of his products. Unlike some of his competitors who exaggerated product features to secure quick sales, Suresh remained truthful, only sharing the genuine benefits of his products. This honesty built a strong foundation of trust with his customers, who began to rely on him for accurate and transparent information. Whenever a new product was introduced, his customers would reach out to Suresh first. This integrity and honesty became the key to his long-term success. Today, his network marketing business continues to grow, and his customers remain loyal because of the trust he has cultivated.

Lesson: Honesty and ethical practices create a loyal customer base that supports long-term success. While taking shortcuts may yield immediate results, ethical business practices foster lasting relationships and stability.

Building Trust with Customers and Team Members

Trust is the foundation of any successful business, and it is especially crucial in network marketing. When customers and team members trust you, they are more likely to remain loyal and engage in repeat business. Trust is built by being transparent, honest, and fulfilling promises consistently. A strong, trustworthy relationship with your customers and team members creates a solid base for your business to grow.

When you establish trust, it leads to a lasting partnership that ensures the longevity of your network marketing business. People want to work with those they trust, and ethical behavior creates a stable environment where that trust can thrive.

Real-Life Story: Manish Pandit from Kanpur, Uttar Pradesh, built a successful network marketing business by being open and honest with his team. He never hesitated to help his team members and always admitted when he made mistakes. This transparency fostered a deep sense of trust among his team, which led to their success. His team worked together through challenges because they trusted Manish to lead them fairly and honestly. This strong bond of trust became the foundation of his business success.

Lesson: Trust may take time to build, but once established, it becomes the foundation for long-term relationships. By maintaining honesty and transparency, you can create lasting bonds with your team and customers, leading to sustained growth.

Building a Business the Right Way

In network marketing, building a business the right way means presenting your products and opportunities without misleading information or false promises. While some may be tempted to exaggerate for quick gains, such practices often lead to failure in the long run.

When you honestly present the benefits of your products, people are more likely to trust you, and this trust forms the foundation of your business. Ethical business practices not only build a strong and sustainable network but also ensure long-term success.

Real-Life Story: Nitin Sharma, upon starting his network marketing journey, noticed that many leaders were making exaggerated claims to secure quick sales. Nitin decided to take a different route, focusing on building his business with honesty and integrity. He always provided accurate information and managed expectations. Over time, Nitin's honesty attracted a loyal customer base and a dedicated team. His ethical approach built a stable and growing business that flourished over time.

Lesson: Building a business with integrity enhances your credibility and reputation. Taking shortcuts may offer short-term benefits, but ethical practices ensure long-term stability and success.

The Importance of Ethics for Long-Term Success

Adhering to ethics is essential for long-term success in network marketing. When you operate with honesty, your business becomes stable and trusted. This trust solidifies your standing as a reliable leader, and your ethical conduct fosters loyalty among both customers and team members.

Ethics not only provide personal satisfaction, but they also establish a strong foundation for your business. When customers and team members trust you, they will continue to work with you, ensuring lasting success. While unethical practices may bring short-term gains, working with integrity ensures lasting, sustainable success.

Real-Life Story: Anil Acharya from Cuttack, Odisha, achieved success in network marketing by maintaining an ethical approach, even when others around him resorted to dishonest tactics. Anil never made false promises and always provided honest, accurate information. As a result, his business became stronger over time, and his team members trusted him completely. Today, Anil is a successful network marketing leader, supported by a loyal team that values his integrity.

Lesson: Ethics and honesty are key to long-term success. Trust is built on truth, and ethical practices lead to stability and sustainable business growth.

Conclusion

Ethics and honesty are the cornerstones of long-term success in network marketing. By adhering to ethical business practices, you build trust with customers and team members, fostering lasting relationships. When you operate with integrity, your business becomes stable and you establish yourself as a reliable and trustworthy leader.

Remember, success is not just about immediate financial gain—it's about building a business based on ethical principles that lead to sustained success. When you follow the right path, success will naturally follow.

Reflective Questions for Personal and Business Growth

1. **Testing Your Ethics:**
   - Do you always act with honesty toward your customers and team members?
   - Have you ever provided misleading information about your products or opportunities? If so, how can this be corrected?
2. **Building Trust in Business:**
   - Do your customers and team members trust you? How do you maintain that trust?

- Do you regularly communicate with your customers and team members, listen to their concerns, and provide solutions?

3. **Following Ethical Business Practices:**
   - Are you following ethical practices in every aspect of your business?
   - Do you teach the importance of ethics to your team members and customers?
4. **Steps to Long-Term Success:**
   - Are your long-term goals built on a foundation of ethical business practices?
   - Are you building long-term relationships with your customers and team members?

Final Message

"Honesty and ethics are the foundation of any successful business."

When you build your business on truth and integrity, you not only achieve immediate success but also lay the groundwork for long-term success. Success is not solely defined by financial gain—it is measured by your moral values and the strength of your integrity. When you follow the right path, success will come naturally.

17

Importance of Personal Branding in Network Marketing

Personal branding in network marketing is the key to standing out from the crowd. In today's digital age, your identity becomes your brand, and the credibility of this brand determines your success. Personal branding is all about how people perceive you and your work. Your brand must be trustworthy, effective, and inspiring.

In this chapter, we will explore the significance of personal branding in network marketing, how to position yourself as a credible and effective brand, and real-life success stories showcasing how personal branding leads to success.

What is Personal Branding and Why is it Important?

Personal branding in network marketing refers to how people perceive your personality, work, and approach. A strong personal brand differentiates you from others and builds trust with your customers and team. To create an impactful brand, first clarify your identity—who you are, what your purpose is, and how you can provide value to others.

Maintain a strong social media presence, share your thoughts, experiences, and success stories regularly. Honesty and transparency are crucial, as they help build trust. When your image is positive, inspiring, and trustworthy, people are naturally drawn to you, helping you grow your network and business.

Real-Life Story: Ravinder Kumar Sharma, a network marketer from Bihar, struggled to grow his team and client base. Realizing that focusing solely on products wasn't enough, he decided to work on his personal branding. Through social media, he began sharing his experiences, success tips, and inspirational stories. His posts were honest and useful, which attracted followers. As Ravinder's social media presence grew, so did his network marketing business. He became successful not only due to his skills but because of his credible personal image and branding.

Learning: Personal branding helps people remember you and your ideas. When you create an effective and trustworthy brand, the number of people connecting with you increases rapidly, providing stability to your business.

Presenting Yourself as an Effective and Trustworthy Brand

To present yourself as a credible and trustworthy brand, consistency in your personal image and work is essential. People should clearly understand who you are, what you do, and the quality of your work.

Trustworthy branding means people connect with you because they trust the information and services you provide. Always provide accurate and useful information. Fulfill your commitments and treat your customers and team members with honesty to increase your credibility. When people see you as a reliable and steady person, they are more likely to stay with you long-term.

Real-Life Story: Vikrant Mehta from Ahmedabad noticed that many network marketers made big promises without maintaining a credible image. He decided to be different by presenting himself as authentic and honest. He consistently shared truthful and accurate information on his social media platforms, avoiding exaggerated promises. Gradually, this honesty-built trust, and his customer base and team began to grow, leading to his business success.

Learning: Maintaining honesty and authenticity in your personal branding builds trust and keeps people connected with you for the long term. A credible image is key to your business's success.

Building a Personal Brand on Social Media

Social media is the most powerful tool for personal branding today. Platforms like Facebook, Instagram, and LinkedIn allow you to create a strong identity. To build your brand, first understand the image you want to project. Keep your target audience in mind and ensure your posts are clear, truthful, and relevant. Share inspirational and valuable content like success stories, product information, and personal experiences regularly.

Ensure that your profile and posts are professional and consistent. Engagement is key—respond to comments and messages, and interact with your followers personally. When people see your brand as honest, trustworthy, and helpful, they are more likely to connect with you and your products.

Real-Life Story: Sonu Jaiswal from Bhopal created a personal brand on Instagram to grow his network marketing business. He consistently shared his experiences, success stories, and inspirational posts. By providing accurate information and avoiding exaggeration, Sonu built trust among his followers. Over time, his follower count grew, and so did his business. His personal branding laid the foundation for his success.

Learning: Social media is a powerful medium. When used effectively and consistently, it helps you build a strong personal brand. Sharing content with honesty and inspiration helps you connect with people and grow your business faster.

Effective Strategies for Personal Branding

To build an effective personal brand, focus on these key strategies:

1. **Clarify Your Brand Identity:** Define who you are, what you do, and what sets you apart. Clarity strengthens your brand and helps people understand your values.
2. **Consistency is Key:** Personal branding is a continuous effort. Regularly post on social media, share experiences, and engage with followers. This consistency builds trust and credibility.
3. **Emphasize Honesty and Transparency:** Always provide accurate information and maintain transparency. This fosters trust, which leads to long-term relationships with your followers.
4. **Incorporate Motivation and Positivity:** People are drawn to those who inspire them. Infuse your brand with positivity and motivation to connect with your audience on a deeper level.

Real-Life Story: Rahul Gupta from Jhansi took a strategic approach to personal branding. He started posting weekly videos covering various aspects of network marketing, including business tips and inspirational stories. His posts were consistent, practical, and inspiring, which helped him attract new leads and team members. This strategy established Rahul as a credible and influential personality, leading to the rapid growth of his business.

Learning: Develop a clear strategy for personal branding and work on it consistently. Whether through videos, blogs, or social media posts, ensure your content is authentic and credible to build trust and attract more people to your network.

Conclusion

Personal branding is crucial for success in network marketing. When you present yourself as a credible and effective brand, people trust you and are more willing to work with you. By using the right strategies on social media and other platforms, you can not only grow your brand but also strengthen it.

Remember, personal branding is the soul of your business. When people trust you and your brand, your chances of success increase significantly.

Reflective Questions for Personal and Business Growth

1. **Evaluating Your Personal Branding:**
    - Do people recognize you as a unique, effective, and credible person?

2. **Your Branding Approach:**
   - Do you post regularly on social media, and do your posts reflect your brand?
   - Do your followers believe in your work and ideas? How do you inspire them?
3. **Branding Strategy:**
   - Is your branding strategy clear and consistent?
   - Do you maintain regularity and accuracy in your branding content?
4. **Improving Your Branding:**
   - Is your branding based on honesty and transparency?
   - Are there any changes you feel are necessary to make your branding more effective?

Final Message

"Your personal branding is your greatest identity."

Your personality, thoughts, and actions shape your brand. When people believe in your brand, they connect with you and contribute to your success.

"Success follows when you lead with honesty and authenticity. Build your brand with integrity, and success will follow."

18

Strategies for Long-Term Success in Network Marketing

Success in network marketing isn't about short-term results; it's about building a sustainable career through long-term strategies. Consistency, planning, and continuous growth are crucial to thriving in this industry. To achieve long-term success, you need to set clear goals, constantly learn, expand your network and team, and maintain a healthy balance between your personal and professional life.

In this chapter, we will explore strategies for long-term success and share real-life examples of individuals who have succeeded using these principles.

Creating Goals and Plans for Long-Term Success

To achieve lasting success, it is essential to create clear, actionable goals and a comprehensive plan. Rather than focusing on short-term gains, think about where you want your business to be in the coming years. This vision allows you to set both long-term and short-term goals, providing direction and keeping you motivated even during challenging times.

By setting clear goals, you can prioritize effectively and make the most of your time. A long-term vision will help guide your daily actions, making sure you are always moving in the right direction toward lasting success.

Real-Life Story: Surendra Kumar Sunny from Jhansi, Madhya Pradesh, initially focused only on immediate sales and quick profits. But over time, he realized the importance of long-term planning. Surendra developed a five-year plan to grow his network marketing business steadily. He set goals to build a new team each year and steadily increase his income. Along the way, he also focused on short-term targets, such as adding new customers monthly and improving his team's training.

Through hard work and a clear vision, Surendra's business grew, and today he leads a successful network that spans across India.

Learning: Long-term goals provide stability and direction. When you look at your business from a long-term perspective and create a detailed plan, your chances of success increase. Consistency and clear direction are essential for long-term success.

Continuous Learning and Growth

In network marketing, continuous learning is essential for success. The industry is ever-evolving, with new technologies, strategies, and customer demands emerging all the time. Only those who stay updated and adapt to these changes can achieve lasting success.

The learning process never stops. To succeed, you must regularly upgrade your skills, knowledge, and approach. When you demonstrate a commitment to learning, your team and customers will look to you as a source of inspiration. Those who are willing to learn and adapt quickly will always have an edge.

Real-Life Story: Radhika, a successful network marketer, never stopped learning. She regularly attended seminars, read up on the latest marketing techniques, and adopted new strategies to stay ahead of her competitors. Radhika knew that staying updated in a fast-changing industry was crucial for long-term success.

Her commitment to learning kept her one step ahead, and her business continued to thrive as she incorporated new ideas and improved her approach.

Learning: Continuous learning is the foundation of long-term success. By constantly improving your knowledge and skills, you not only boost your business but also become a role model for others.

Expanding Your Network and Team

In network marketing, your success is closely tied to the size and strength of your team. A larger, more effective team increases your chances of long-term success. Continuously adding new members to your network is essential for business growth, but it's equally important to support and guide them.

Train your team, share business insights, and encourage them to grow. The more successful your team members become, the stronger your network will be. Stay connected with your team, address their concerns, and keep them motivated. Building a loyal and motivated team is key to sustained growth.

Real-Life Story: Biswajit Dutta from Tinsukia, Assam, adopted a simple yet effective strategy to expand his network. He organized monthly seminars to share product information and promote the benefits of network marketing. He also invited successful business leaders to speak, which inspired new members. His focus was not only on selling products but also on guiding new recruits and helping them succeed.

Over time, Biswajit's team grew steadily, and his business flourished as new members joined every month.

Learning: For long-term success, it is essential to continually grow and strengthen your team. Your team is your greatest asset, and nurturing it is the key to lasting achievement.

Maintaining Personal and Professional Balance

Balancing your personal and professional life is crucial for long-term success. Network marketing can be time-consuming, and focusing solely on business can negatively impact your personal life, leading to stress and burnout. On the other hand, neglecting your business in favor of personal matters can stall your progress.

A successful network marketer is someone who can balance both aspects of life effectively. Proper time management is essential. Dedicate specific time slots to work and personal activities. When you work, stay focused, and when spending time with family, be fully present.

Real-Life Story: Varun Patil from Nanded, Maharashtra, struggled to maintain a balance between his family and business. He realized that if he wanted long-term success, he needed to find harmony between the two. Varun began managing his time better and dedicated equal attention to both his business and personal life.

This balanced approach not only helped his business grow but also brought happiness and peace into his family life.

Learning: Maintaining a healthy balance between your personal and professional life is crucial for long-term success. A well-balanced life helps you stay focused and motivated, while also ensuring your well-being.

Conclusion

Long-term success in network marketing is the result of strategic planning, continuous learning, growing your network, and maintaining a balance between work and personal life. Achieving success in this industry requires patience, persistence, and the right strategies.

Network marketing offers tremendous opportunities for long-term success, but only for those who follow the right path and stay committed to their goals.

Reflective Questions for Personal and Business Growth

1. **Long-Term Goals and Plans:**
   - Have you set clear goals for the next five years in your network marketing business?
   - Are your goals balanced between short-term and long-term objectives?
2. **Continuous Learning Process:**
   - Are you regularly learning new marketing strategies and techniques?

- Do you participate in seminars, workshops, or online courses to update your knowledge?

3. **Network and Team Expansion:**
   - Are you adding new members to your team or network each month?
   - Do you have strategies in place to keep your team motivated and growing?

4. **Personal and Professional Balance:**
   - Are you maintaining a balance between your personal and professional life?
   - Are you managing your time effectively to ensure harmony in both areas?

Final Message

"Long-term success is a journey made up of small, consistent efforts."

Success doesn't come overnight—it requires constant learning, hard work, and patience. Your small efforts today lay the foundation for bigger achievements tomorrow. Keep expanding your network, balance your personal and professional life, and improve yourself each day. With persistence and dedication, you can achieve your long-term goals.

19

Key Tips for Success in Network Marketing

Network marketing is a business that thrives on persistence, consistent effort, and implementing the right strategies. Throughout this book, we have discussed the essential elements required to become a successful network marketer. We've explored how cultivating the right mindset, setting clear goals, fostering teamwork, leveraging the power of duplication, and mastering follow-up techniques can significantly boost your success.

The key to succeeding lies in maintaining consistency in your hard work, believing in your potential, and adopting a long-term perspective.

Important Guidance for Long-Term Success

Achieving long-term success in network marketing is not easy, but it is absolutely possible. The most successful individuals in this business are those who never stop learning and consistently strive to expand their knowledge. In network marketing, your team and network are your biggest assets, so it's crucial to keep your team motivated and maintain strong, positive relationships with them. Additionally, having a clear goal is essential—knowing where you want to go helps you work more effectively toward that destination.

Only those who demonstrate patience and consistency ultimately achieve long-term success in this industry. Hard work, a willingness to learn, and a clear sense of direction can lead you to success in network marketing.

Real-Life Story: Hrithik Avasthi from Mumbai faced numerous challenges when he first started in network marketing. He heard "no" more times than he could count and often felt discouraged. However, instead of giving up, Hrithik reassessed his goals and resolved to keep trying. He focused on motivating his team and took small, steady steps to grow his business.

Hrithik made it a point to network consistently, meeting new people, and providing the right guidance to his team. Slowly but surely, his efforts began to pay off. His team started growing, and his business stabilized. Today, Hrithik is a successful network marketer with a flourishing business.

Learning: Consistency and patience are critical for long-term success. No matter how many setbacks you face, if you continue moving forward with determination, success will eventually follow. Failure is simply a temporary stop on the journey, but persistence and progress are the keys to lasting achievement.

20

Final Message to Keep Moving Forward

There are no shortcuts to success in network marketing. It is a journey that demands continuous hard work. You must keep connecting with new people, expanding your network, and nurturing strong relationships with your team. Success comes only through sustained effort, patience, and the ability to work in the right direction. Both time and effort are necessary ingredients.

Real success in network marketing is achieved by those who diligently work on building connections, maintaining consistency, and pursuing their goals with dedication. In this business, the support of your team and your ability to guide them effectively will drive you forward.

Inspirational Message: Sonu Sharma was a young network marketer who faced numerous failures early in his career. Despite the setbacks, he never gave up. He viewed each failure as a learning experience and moved forward with patience. Over time, Sonu began to understand the core principles of network marketing. He realized that hard work, patience, and the right strategies are essential for success in this business.

Sonu focused on building trusting relationships with his customers and team members. His goal was not just to make sales, but to understand people's needs and provide solutions. By consistently motivating his team and offering the right guidance, his network grew significantly.

Today, Sonu's network marketing business is thriving, and he is recognized as a successful leader. His journey inspires others, showing them the path to success through perseverance and dedication.

Learning: In network marketing, patience, hard work, and building trust are crucial for success. True success comes from learning from failures, forming strong relationships, and working steadily in the right direction.

Key Takeaways:

1. **Consistency and Persistence:** Success in network marketing is a journey, not a destination. You must consistently put in the effort, connect with new people, and support your team to see real results.
2. **Learning and Growth:** Continuous learning is the key to staying relevant in the industry. Always be open to new strategies, trends, and ways to improve both personally and professionally.
3. **Teamwork and Support:** Your team is your greatest asset in network marketing. Work on building relationships based on trust and provide the guidance they need to succeed.

4. **Patience and Long-Term Vision:** Success doesn't happen overnight. A long-term vision, combined with daily actions toward that goal, will lead you to success over time.

There is no fast track to success in network marketing, but there is a proven path. It involves consistent hard work, maintaining strong relationships, and moving forward with patience and dedication. When you focus on these fundamental principles, long-term success is not only possible but inevitable.

Network marketing is not just about selling products; it's the art of building strong relationships with people. When you create meaningful and trusting connections, people are more likely to trust you and enjoy working with you. This leads to greater success.

21

Essential Tips for Long-Term Success in Network Marketing

1. **Believe in Yourself:** Your mindset is the foundation of your success. Trust in your abilities and stay confident in your potential.
2. **Maintain Consistency:** Success in network marketing is built on consistent effort. Take small, steady steps forward every day.
3. **Keep Your Team Motivated:** Your team is your greatest asset. Support and encourage them so they can also achieve success.
4. **Keep Learning:** Always strive to learn something new. Continuous learning fuels both personal and professional growth.
5. **Build Strong Customer Relationships:** Your relationship with your customers is the cornerstone of your business. Strengthen it with honesty and transparency.

6. **Maintain a Positive Attitude:** Challenges are part of the journey. Face them with a positive outlook and turn obstacles into opportunities.
7. **Manage Time Effectively:** Balance between your personal and professional life is key to long-term progress.
8. **Expand Your Network:** The more contacts you make, the more opportunities arise. Keep expanding your network.
9. **Understand Your Product:** Knowledge is power. Understand the features and benefits of your product so you can share it confidently and accurately.
10. **Develop Leadership Skills:** Success in network marketing requires you to be both a good salesperson and a strong leader. Guide your team effectively.
11. **Give Positive Feedback:** Encouraging your team through positive feedback boosts their confidence and unlocks their potential.
12. **Set Clear Goals:** Clear goals provide direction. Both short-term and long-term goals help keep you and your team focused.
13. **Communicate Effectively:** Clear and inspiring communication is essential. Stay engaged with your team and customers, and offer solutions when needed.
14. **Focus on Personal Branding:** Establish your identity on social media and other platforms to attract people to your business.
15. **Stay Goal-Oriented:** Keep your long-term and short-term goals in mind. If you encounter challenges, adjust your strategy—don't give up on the goal.
16. **Be Patient:** Network marketing success doesn't happen overnight. Celebrate small victories and stay committed to learning.

17. **Cultivate a Positive Mindset:** Avoid negativity. A positive mindset enhances your energy and motivation.
18. **Maintain Transparency:** Honesty in all aspects of your business builds long-term trust and success.
19. **Attend Networking Events:** Participate in seminars and networking events to generate new ideas and make valuable connections.
20. **Accept Criticism Positively:** Constructive criticism is a tool for improvement. Embrace it and use it to grow.
21. **Leverage Technology:** Utilize modern tools and social media to expand your reach and stay connected with your team and customers.
22. **Create a Financial Plan:** Manage your income wisely and create a financial plan to prepare for uncertainties.
23. **Stay Open to New Ideas:** Marketing strategies evolve. Stay informed of new trends and incorporate innovative ideas into your business.
24. **Understand Customer Needs:** Provide solutions tailored to your customers' needs. Excellent customer service is the backbone of success.
25. **Create a Positive Work Environment:** A positive, supportive atmosphere energizes your team and improves results.
26. **Learn from Failure:** Failure teaches valuable lessons. View setbacks as opportunities to improve and move forward.
27. **Prioritize Health and Well-Being:** Physical and mental health are essential to sustaining success. Incorporate exercise, meditation, or yoga into your routine to stay energized.
28. **Provide Value to Customers:** Focus on delivering value through your products and services. When customers see real benefits, they will stay loyal to your brand.

29. **Organize Training and Workshops:** Regular training helps your team stay up-to-date with the latest strategies and improve performance.
30. **Adopt a Long-Term View:** Don't expect immediate success. Network marketing is a long-term journey that requires patience and sustained effort.
31. **Use Your Product:** Use the product or service you're selling. Personal experience allows you to speak authentically about its benefits.
32. **Focus on Planning and Strategy:** Set weekly, monthly, and yearly plans for achieving your goals, and work steadily towards them.

By adopting these tips, you'll strengthen your foundation for long-lasting success in network marketing. When you believe in yourself and work diligently, you can face every challenge with confidence. Building strong, trustworthy relationships with your customers and team will further solidify your business. Continuous learning will keep you evolving, ensuring that your success lasts not just in the present but for years to come.

22

Final Reflection Questions for Business & Personal Growth

The questions below are designed to help you deeply reflect on your network marketing journey and identify areas for growth and improvement. Answer these questions honestly and thoughtfully, as they form the foundation for your continued success:

Self-Belief:

- *Question*: Do you genuinely believe in your ability to succeed in network marketing?
- *Question*: How do you maintain confidence when faced with challenges?

Consistency and Effort:

- *Question*: Are you consistent in your daily efforts to grow your business?

- *Question*: What steps do you take to improve your daily routine and sustain consistent effort?

Team Motivation:

- *Question*: How do you ensure your team stays motivated and energized?
- *Question*: What strategies do you use to help your team achieve their goals?

Continuous Learning:

- *Question*: Are you consistently seeking opportunities to learn new strategies and skills?
- *Question*: In what areas do you need to expand your knowledge to advance in your business?

Relationship Building:

- *Question*: Do you have strong, trusting relationships with your customers and team members?
- *Question*: How can you further strengthen and deepen these relationships?

Time Management:

- *Question*: Are you effectively balancing your personal and professional life?
- *Question*: How can you improve your time management to achieve both personal and professional success?

Networking and Expansion:

- *Question*: Are you actively expanding your network and connecting with new people?

- *Question*: What new approaches can you try to grow your network more effectively?

Product Knowledge:

- *Question*: Do you have a thorough understanding of the products you sell?
- *Question*: How can you enhance your product knowledge to better serve your customers?

Leadership Development:

- *Question*: Are you continually developing your leadership skills?
- *Question*: How can you help your team members develop their own leadership potential?

Goal Setting:

- *Question*: Have you set clear, long-term goals for your business?
- *Question*: How can you break down these long-term goals into smaller, actionable tasks?

Feedback and Growth:

- *Question*: Do you embrace feedback from your team and customers with a positive attitude?
- *Question*: What steps can you take to grow and improve based on the feedback you receive?

Branding and Personal Image:

- *Question*: Are you consistently working on building your personal brand?

- *Question*: Does your brand accurately reflect your values, personality, and authenticity?

Innovation and Adaptation:

- *Question*: Are you open to new ideas and adaptable to changes in the market?
- *Question*: What innovative strategies can you implement to improve your business?

Patience and Perseverance:

- *Question*: How do you maintain patience and motivation during slow business periods?
- *Question*: What methods do you use to stay focused on your long-term goals?

Health and Wellness:

- *Question*: Are you taking care of your physical and mental well-being while growing your business?
- *Question*: How can you improve your work-life balance to ensure long-term success and personal well-being?

Conclusion

Answering these questions will help you assess your progress and identify key areas for improvement. Reflect on your answers, and use these insights to continue growing both personally and professionally as you advance in your network marketing journey.

Concluding Thoughts

Network marketing opens doors to unlimited opportunities. It is not merely a business but a powerful vehicle to transform your dreams into reality. Your success in this industry is built on hard work, dedication, and the right mindset. The journey may not always be easy or straightforward, but those with the courage and determination to keep moving forward will ultimately reach their destination.

Mahatma Gandhi's inspiring quote, *"Be the change you want to see in the world,"* is highly relevant in network marketing. If you embody the positive change you want to see in others, you will rise to new heights in your business. Every challenge on this path will make you stronger, and before you know it, you will have reached the point you envisioned when you began.

Your success will not only reflect your personal growth but also serve as a beacon of inspiration to your team, clients, and the broader network marketing community. Remember, true victory in network marketing is not only measured by profits but also by the positive impact you create through your efforts. By continuously developing yourself and helping others achieve their dreams, you experience success that brings a deeper sense of fulfillment and pride.

In Conclusion

The goal of this book was not only to inspire but to provide you with a deep understanding of the many facets of network marketing. We've covered the principles of success in simple, practical ways, making it easier for you to implement them in your life and business.

Now, it's up to you to apply these principles and strategies to your network marketing journey. Remember, success is not a destination but a journey that requires continuous movement, persistence, and learning. Your hard work, dedication, and patience will lead you to success.

Often, we dream of the destination where success and recognition await, but seldom do we acknowledge the personal growth that occurs along the way. Network marketing is not just about building a business; it's about building yourself. Every day, you become a little stronger, wiser, and more experienced.

Yes, you will face difficulties—rejections, setbacks, and moments of doubt. But understand that failure is not the end—it's a stepping stone. Every "no" brings you closer to the "yes" that will open the doors to your success. It is your patience and resilience that will set you apart from others.

You now have everything you need to succeed in network marketing. You've learned how to build a team, foster trust with clients, manage your time effectively, and apply consistent effort. The next step is simple: take action.

Your success is in your hands. The moment you take that first step, your journey toward success begins. While the destination may seem distant, each small effort you make brings you closer. In time, you will find that success comes naturally to those who work hard and stay committed.

No journey is without its challenges, and to achieve greatness, we must often step outside our comfort zones. But rest assured, when you work with honesty, passion, and persistence, success will come. Every small step you take is progress toward the big goal you've always envisioned.

With the knowledge gained from this book, you are now equipped to succeed in network marketing. But remember—knowledge only holds value when it is applied. Starting today, turn your dreams into reality. Move forward with renewed confidence and passion, and success will surely follow.

Success is within your grasp—take the step, and the destination will meet you.

Regards

Surya Sinha
Suryasinha101@gmail.com

Network marketing is not just a job; it's a lifestyle. You choose how to invest your time, effort, and energy. It gives you the opportunity to be your own boss, work with your team, and improve your financial situation. In this field, you live life on your own terms.

Real-Life Stories

Here are some testimonials that showcase how the teachings and network marketing training provided by **Mr. Surya Sinha** have opened up new paths of success for distributors and customers alike. These stories illustrate how they successfully built their careers in network marketing and developed into outstanding leaders:

Vikas Gupta, Kolkata (Network Leader)- *"Dear Mahaguru Shri Surya Sinha Ji, I am writing this letter to express my deep gratitude to you. You are truly a great guru, whose compassion and spirit of service is unmatched. Your selfless dedication has empowered so many people, including myself, and given me the direction I needed to succeed. Without your guidance, I would never have become a successful network leader. I am forever grateful to you."*

Manish Kumar, Nagpur (Network Leader)- *"Dear Mahaguru Shri Surya Sinha Ji, your teachings and techniques have been with me every step of the way. You showed me how to achieve success in network marketing, guiding me to become an effective leader. Your strategies taught me that hard work alone* *is not enough—strategy and approach matter, too. Whatever success I have today is because of your guidance. I thank you from the bottom of my heart."*

Deepak Yadav, Kanpur (Leader and Network Builder)- *"Dear Mahaguru Ji, your teachings have completely transformed my journey in network marketing. Before meeting you, I was directionless. Your clear vision and strong strategies helped me succeed. You taught me how to build and manage a strong network. I owe my success as a leader and distributor to your wisdom. I express my deepest gratitude to you."*

Sandeep Gupta, Bhopal (Successful Distributor)- *"Dear Mahaguru Shri Surya Sinha Ji, every moment spent with you has brought light into my life. Before your training, I did not understand the complexities of network marketing, but you taught me simple and effective strategies that changed my life. I credit all my success to the strategies you taught me. Without your guidance, none of this would have been possible, and for that, I am truly grateful."*

Avinash Chaudhary, Raipur (Successful Leader)- *"Dear Mahaguru Shri Surya Sinha Ji, your guidance has completely changed my life. Your training took my network marketing skills to a new level and reignited my self-confidence. Where I once struggled with hesitation, your techniques and motivation gave me the confidence I needed to succeed as a distributor and leader. I will be forever thankful to you for showing me the right path."*

Rakesh Gupta, Patna (Network Leader)- *"Dear Mahaguru Ji, your teachings have shown me that network marketing is not just a business, but an art. Before your training, I was just an ordinary distributor, but your guidance inspired me to become a leader. You taught me the importance of building and leading* *a strong team. Today, I am a successful leader, and I owe my success to your motivation and techniques."*

Monty Singh, Pune (Network Leader)- *"Dear Mahaguru Shri Surya Sinha Ji, your guidance came as a light in my life. Your selfless service and compassion are beyond words. You are not only a great guru but also a true guide who helps others find the path to success. I express my heartfelt gratitude to you and seek your blessings always."*

Mohit Gupta, Delhi (Successful Distributor and Leader)- *"Mahaguru Ji, the training I received from you revolutionized my life. Your techniques made me a successful distributor and an effective leader, helping me take my network to great heights. You taught me the principles of business and showed me the path to success. I am deeply grateful and seek your blessings throughout my life."*

Anil Sharma, Jaipur (Successful Leader)- *"Dear Mahaguru Shri Surya Sinha Ji, I never considered network marketing before, but your teachings changed my perspective. Your training showed me how success can be achieved in this business. Today, I am a successful distributor and leader, and for this, I thank you from the bottom of my heart."*

Sumit Agarwal, Lucknow (Network Leader)- *"Mahaguru Ji, your training helped me understand the deep principles of network marketing. You taught me how to become an effective leader and how to build and motivate a strong network. Today, my team and I are reaching new heights of success, and I owe it all to you."*

Pallavi Gupta, Patna (Network Leader)- *"Dear Mahaguru Ji, your training opened my eyes to the true art of network marketing. The strategies you taught me helped me become a* *successful leader, giving me the confidence I needed to succeed. Today, I am thriving in my network, and I thank you deeply for your guidance."*

These powerful testimonials demonstrate how **Mr. Surya Sinha's** training has transformed the lives and careers of many individuals. His unique approach and deep understanding have helped countless people not only excel in network marketing but also create a lasting impact in their personal and professional lives.

Many of these individuals attribute their growth in confidence, leadership, and marketing skills to **Mr. Sinha's** training, proving that with the right guidance, anyone can achieve success in network marketing. These stories serve as a beacon of inspiration for those striving to make their mark in this industry.

Narender Kumar Verma
Publisher, Diamond Books

A Humble Request

From the bottom of my heart, I humbly request that if you found this book valuable, please share it with your friends, family, and colleagues. This book isn't just about sharing knowledge; it's about sharing the immense possibilities of network marketing. By sharing this book, you could help change someone's life.

Spread the word on social media, and let more people benefit from the lessons and inspiration contained within these pages. Together, we can inspire others and help them achieve their dreams. Your effort in sharing this book will be a true blessing, knowing that you have played a part in transforming someone's life.

Regards

Surya Sinha
Suryasinha101@gmail.com

DIAMOND BOOKS PRESENTS

Internationally Renowned Best Selling Author, Human Trainer & Motivator

SURYA SINHA'S BOOKS

Available in Hindi, English, Bengali, Gujarati, Marathi & All Other Indian Languages

DIAMOND BOOKS X-30, Okhla Industrial Area, Phase-II New Delhi-110020
Ph: 011-40712200 email : wecare@diamondbooks.in www.diamondbooks.in